Spirit Guides:
We Are Not Alone

Spirit Guides

Iris Belhayes
with **Enid**

Cover design by Maria Kay Simms
San Diego, California

Printed in the United States of America

Published by ACS Publications
P.O. Box 34487
San Diego, CA 92163-4487

First Printing, May 1986
Eleventh Printing, September 1994

Library of Congress Cataloging-in-Publication Data

Belhayes, Iris, 1935-
  Spirit guides.

  Includes index.
  1. Spirit writings.   I. Title.
BF1301.B378 1986   133.9'3   86-7866
ISBN 0-917086-80-5 (pbk.)

Dedication

This book is dedicated to
those who can see and those
who want to see beyond the
"accepted vision."

Contents

Preface

Enid is a spirit who has experienced many incarnations on this planet and now having completed her travels upon our earth, has decided to communicate from her plane of existence to ours with the purpose of helping us through the trials of awakening. Her purpose as stated to me, is to make the spirit world an easy and safe place to reach toward and to help us understand our spirit guides and how they fit into our lives. She is also intensely interested in our very real connection to our inner beingness, our higher self.

My experience with Enid has been uniquely special and spiritually rewarding. I am truly her student and she is my teacher. We met first while I was trying to write a novel. There were distinct impressions being received that did not fit that context.

The idea for writing a book about **Spirit Guides** came to me and there she was saying, "I'll do it with you!". Needless to say, I was delighted and excited and a little fearful all at once, but laying aside my anxiety, I ran to the typewriter and this book is the result.

Communication with my own **Spirit Guides** began in 1974 but I had never read anything about them and was not even involved in the psychic world. Enid is not my spirit guide in the sense that is described in this book, but is a special "teacher" who has decided to come **through** me, not merely **to** me. She wishes to guide us all with this book. She tells me there are more to come and her public messages attest to that.

I never "felt" Enid with my body, nor did I "feel" her emotionally, although I was sometimes greatly moved emotionally by concepts that came through in the writing. There were times I became swept up in the energy of her communications and felt exhilarated by them, but Enid never impinged upon or moved into my body.

After finishing this book, however, I experienced Enid in a different way. She came much closer and began to speak directly through me in a delightfully old-fashioned Irish accent. She opens my eyes, gestures with my hands and body, walks around giving hugs and kisses and drinks water occasionally. She is warm, understanding and funny. I love her deeply.

I have helped others discover their *spirit guides*, and my experience is very different from that that I have with Enid. I can feel the *guides* of others as they enter the electrical field of my body. My feeling is always of excitement and joy. The experience is wonderful, reassuring and never frightening. At those times I also am able to view, as it were, the *inner beingness* of the person in front of me, and I feel blessed in a special way and always feel honored. I am able at such times to briefly glimpse the beauty, purity and true energy thrust behind or beyond the body of the person sitting there. I see them free of all earthly personality and problems. It is a rare and wonderful experience and I am always struck by the exquisite wonder that I see in them.

It is not so important that our *guides* are watching over us, but that we learn to perceive them. We gain the ability to evoke their presence or attention for ourselves. At such times, in my own experience, I am communicating, perceiving and experiencing across exciting dimensions and into stunning realities.

Perhaps the greatest value of our *spirit guides* lies in the fact that they really do exist and that they exist **outside** our earthly reality, yet are able to bridge the difference. We, in turn, learn to bridge the difference when we are able to send and receive communication with them. In this way do our worlds meet and that fulfills their purpose.

Never in my life have I believed in some deep, hidden evil in humankind. I must say that what I have viewed in others only reinforces my belief in the deep and sometimes hidden beauty and purity that is the heritage of us all.

It is my hope that this book will inspire and help those who wish to enrich the experience of their own *knowingness* and to meet the *inner self* — inner voice — and the inner beauty that is there for the finding.

Iris Belhayes

REG#01   BOOKSELLER#037
RECEIPT# 12974 05/29/96   8:07 PM

CUSTOMER COPY

S 0917086805   SPIRIT GOES
1 @ 12.95   12.95

S 1883753240   LOSING YOUR MIND
1 @ 14.95   14.95

SUBTOTAL   27.90
SALES TAX - 6%   1.67
TOTAL   29.57
VISA PAYMENT   29.57
ACCOUNT# 4128002113532837   EXP 1296
AUTHORIZATION# 00   CLERK 37

CHAPTER ONE
WHY ARE WE HERE?

We are not alone. We are not floating in a vast sea of unknownness about which we can never know anything. We have not been stuck into a fearful void, landing in a world about which we are not to be given the rules for survival — although it may at times seem as though we have. We are much more knowledgeable about this world than we have ever imagined.

Just as we think before we learn the language, we see before we can focus our eyes — and, sometimes, we see the sounds that comprise physical objects. Sometimes we hear the colors around us. Early in our babyhood we are not yet conditioned to physical symbolization and we are floating in and out and between dimensions. We are also drawing upon other past existences to help with the translations of the symbols of this universe.

Very early, before history as we know it, we retained the ability to keep in touch with other realities, other dimensions, other worlds. Through a series of events and misjudgments and misunderstandings, we have arrived at the present level of unawareness, in which our inner *knowingness* is blocked off to one degree or another. As a result, most *beings* on this plane of existence are convinced that this is the only world there is. They may have some religious-based sense of "life after death," but for the most part they think they **are** their bodies, whereas, they are separate entities who live throughout eternity, experiencing, growing and constantly changing, developing, creating worlds and dimensions of their own.

Humankind has always known or at least felt there was someone out there looking over us... Loving us... Protecting us from the dangers of this "unfriendly" planet. This knowing or feeling has been translated in many ways... ways in which humankind has tried to explain its own existence. Most societies or groups of people have decided that the presence or presences they feel must be connected to a kind of superparent or guardian who watches our actions and judges whether or not we deserve award or punishment.

There are, indeed, *beings* "out there" who care for us but they are not judgmental. They do not deal in punishment neither do they hold one of us above the rest, nor view anyone as being bad or wrong. They see each of us as perfect, playing out life on this plane as best we can with the circumstances we have given ourselves. They understand that each of us is experiencing those things necessary for us to experience in order to fulfill our own thrusts for learning, development, adventure and growth.

Life in the Beginning

Life on this plane is harder than was intended. We originally came armed with much more awareness than is now the case. We could play games here with much more alacrity, excitement, cheerfulness and a lot more *knowingness* than we allow ourselves today. We could consciously travel into one dimension or another at will while still relating to the symbols of this universe — much as one is able to think in more than one language, once a second one is learned. We communicated freely with other species — animals and plants. Our viewpoints were much more varied.

Now, in order to play the game here one must put blinders on and veil the senses so as to be able to agree to it at all. Generation by generation, people began to forget and forget. Viewpoints became more and more fixed on this universe and its symbols.

We put blinders on very much in the way children hide from the truth about Santa Claus. They want it to be true. They enjoy the excitement, mystery and intrigue that is a part of the myth, and they want it to last as long as possible. On one level, they "know" the truth, but on the surface they perpetuate and enhance the game by participating, even sitting on Santa-costumed laps, convincing themselves that the whole thing is real. They do this to such an extent that they cry and feel genuine loss when they finally have to admit there is no Santa Claus. They begin learning this world's lessons very early indeed. Sometimes, the transition works well if they can realize that it is the spirit of Santa that is magical, not the details of landing on rooftops and climbing down chimneys, and that, in truth, Santa Claus really does exist — in the giving part of each of us.

In like manner, we need to learn the same kinds of lessons all through life, seeing things as they really are rather than coming to very negative conclusions. We often forget to look and see where the magic really lies: in our own emotions, actions, awarenesses, viewpoints and in our own causing.

Hiding from the Truth

Now, in order for us to take this universe, planet, society, seriously at all, without doubling up in laughter, we do have to hide from ourselves truths that would lay it all open for us, and we fear that in knowing too much we would lose our game. Not so. There is plenty of game left even with finding out all we can and learning to operate on higher levels of understanding and creation. What hasn't been realized is the extent to which we have hidden truth from ourselves. There is little danger of ruining our games and stopping the show by learning too much.

A prevalent thought is that it is dangerous and even sanity-threatening to look beyond the accepted vision of "truth" as has been decided upon by the masses who respond to the lower spectrums of understanding. Limitations are placed upon society's realities by the masses of unenlightened and frightened persons. The more *enlightened ones* must always be careful not to frighten them more. That is why gentleness and love are the best teachers.

So — why are we here, if we have to close our eyes and minds to the truth in order to be here? Each of us has a set of goals that differ somewhat one to the other. But the basic reasons are multiple.

Why Are We Here?

We are here for the playing of the game of life in physical form.

We are here to learn how to create with thought and emotion.

We are here to learn how to create responsibly — our lives, our relationships, our fulfillment of personal and spiritual growth.

We are here to learn again that we are a part of **All There Is**.

That is a lot to be here for, and we keep coming back until we are satisfied we have completed our goals for experiencing life in physical form. Now, until we have learned all we can from the goals we have laid out for ourselves, we cannot progress to higher states of existence. We are all straining at that membrane that separates our awareness from the glories of deeper spiritual experience.

The Appearance of Separateness

In this world, we play the game of being separate and uninvolved only to learn that there is no such thing. There are many obstacles in this world and separateness is one of the biggest. Our dramatizations of separation, the idea that others are alien to our own experiences, that animals or plants are *beingnesses* totally apart from our knowing, or that other worlds are beyond any perimeters of our responsibility — all these convictions are products wholly of this universe and serve only to perpetuate our differences.

During this dawning of our awakening as a species we will see the strangers in us disappear and the lovely *oneness* of our being open up to let in the light of true love and acceptance of all *life* and *All There Is*.

So these are the lessons we are learning now with every reach, every selfless act of love, every realization of *inner beingness*.

These goals are not, however, selfish and self-oriented goals. When one wins, everyone else wins as well; because we are all a part of *All There Is* and there is no real separation, only a physical universe idea that we are separate. This does not mean that we are not individuals. We are.

> We are part of all creation on every dimension, world or universe. We are involved with all of life and all of creation on every plane of existence.

Life Is Beautiful

Is it not exciting to contemplate the adventure inherent in the search for enlightenment which is our true native condition? We came here for adventure, yet truth and remembering our beginnings become an even greater adventure.

There is absolutely nothing to fear in delving into one's *inner beingness*. There is only truth and beauty to be found there. Any thought we have is safe to think. Any realization we perceive is safe to perceive. Any picture we see is safe to peruse. **Anything** we can become aware of is safe and will lead to enlightenment. There is nothing at all to fear from our own inner reality. Most of our fears are fears of ourselves and what we might find in our own minds.

If we see things we do not immediately understand — see things sitting right there in our own minds that are frightening and inexplicable — if we see things that are unpleasant to us, perhaps dark, ugly pictures and nightmarish dangers, we need only realize that these are events we have **already** experienced and looking at them directly merely gives us the opportunity to reduce their power to frighten. There is **nothing** we cannot face. In some cases we misassess the meaning of those things that lie beneath our ordinary awareness. Our translations are a bit off and we are taking what we see far too seriously. We can lay aside our fears in order to perceive the safety and beauty that lies within our knowing.

With each new realization we come close to the understanding we seek. When we finally do discover the last pieces of the puzzle, we are ready to go on to the next world — the next adventure — the next arena for growth.

Although we are perfect when we arrive in this universe and we are perfect when we leave it, our experiences have enriched our existences. We share what we have learned and seen with each other.

In all worlds we find adventure and rich experience. There is no end to the possibilities for challenge and excitement. When we leave this plane, we will not be going to some kind of boring existence, merely floating around in nothingness. If floating around in nothingness is what you want, of course you can have that.

Any world that can be imagined can exist and probably does. It can exist in great detail. Many times when we imagine wonderful worlds in our daydreams and night dreams, it is because they actually already do exist; and what we think we are imagining is actually recall of the past or future (since time outside a physical universe doesn't exist).

Physical Versus Spiritual

There is, on the one hand, a feverish drive to interiorize deeper and deeper into the physical universe, playing with its symbols, gathering even more symbols, changing them, mutating them and creating new meanings for them. Now, on the other hand, interests in altered states of consciousness, travel out of the body, knowledge of other dimensions, ESP, are also energetically being investigated.

At first and even maybe at second glance, the scientific and spiritual turns of mind are opposites, but they are merely different ways of approaching the same or similar questions. Eventually, the scientist would or could (if the climate were to be one of complete freedom in experimentation and search) come out the other side of the physical and find it all to be spiritual in nature to begin with. Some scientists already have discovered some concepts of that nature.

Those of us who are not scientists, however, have an edge, so to speak, because our barriers are more easily set aside without fear of losing face in the scientific community. One does, however, risk reality gaps with friends and family, and that force can be very strong. It takes courage to look beyond the accepted vision no matter who you are. One can play around with other dimensions and realities in spite of, not with the aid of, the physical universe and its symbols. We don't even have to pretend to be scientific.

Many of our inspirations come directly from our *guides* and this includes our scientist friends. In our own ways we are all scientists of a sort. We are constantly experimenting with one idea or another, even in our sleep. The main difference is that our laboratories are contained in the arena of our everyday lives, our kitchens, playpens, offices and in all our creative moments whether awake or asleep.

The Role of Spirit Guides

One important bridge between this universe and the rest of Life is spanned by our *spirit guides* and *teachers*. *Spirit guides* are old *friends* from the *spirit world*. They are not in body and they are most probably only in the vicinity of this plane and not a part of it. We chose them before taking a body and shared our *life plans* and goals with them as well. They have promised to help us by inspiring us to attain these goals. *Teachers* are *spirit guides* who have agreed to assist us more specifically in areas concerning our reawakening, healing and the arts. It is not the purpose of any of these *guides* to usurp our free will or our abilities to discover enlightenment on our own. *Teachers* very often communicate to us in our sleep as do all our *guides*. When we are in reverie or sleep, we are most receptive to their communications.

Why we need *spirit guides*, especially if we are here to stand upon our own feet and learn these lessons, is here answered. Due to the overwhelming beliefs which have accumulated across "time" as we know it, our awareness as a species has dwindled to small peepholes, visible to a few. There have always been those who seemed to be able to see above the clouds. They are either nearing the fulfillment of their goals here, or they have come purposefully at specific times to help inspire others to look and see what is there beyond the confines of this plane. It is never accidental, just as your own growth is never accidental.

Our *guides* don't try to answer all our questions for us or try to solve all our problems as much as they help us contact our own inner selves. In other words, they validate our own abilities to find answers for ourselves. They guide us to our own *beingness*. That is what is meant by "guiding." It is not meant as guardian angels who swoop down and keep us from getting hurt or killed. This is why we often feel we "know" what our *guides* are going to tell us.

Gently and with great care they direct us to our own *being* so that we gain in the power of our own knowing. If the answer seems foreign or new, it only points to how far we have strayed from our own inner *beingness*.

It is those who are more aware who bear the responsibility of encouraging others to "see." It is the burden of the more aware to be understanding and compassionate with those who are not ready to look beyond the game of this plane to the wonders in store for all of us. *Spirit guides* work directly through you and through others who are more aware, to help you open up to the *Real Realities*. (*Real Realities* or *Real Reality* describes realities outside this limited universe. Many of the *Real Realities* are reachable in some fashion through greater insight, awareness and growth.)

Those who are more aware are not without their problems. They must grant rightness to those who would invalidate realities other than those with which they are familiar, measurable, visible, touchable and "physical." At the same time, many such people talk of "flying by the seat of my pants" and having that "old gut-feeling" about something and never even connect with the fact that they, too, are "seeing."

Enlightened Ones

Teachers, as we mentioned earlier, are *spirit guides* who help us with specific areas such as awakening, healing and the arts or other creative endeavors. Many of these *guides* are interested in "taking body" in order to participate more directly in the awakening process. They are sometimes known in the *spirit world* as the *enlightened ones* because they come with more complete connections to their own *inner beingness* and they begin to realize their complete awakening at some point. When they do, they set about fulfilling their goals as *teachers* or ones who inspire others to awaken. They are less interested in being "leaders" or gurus than they are in aiding others to come into their own power.

It is no coincidence that many *teachers* and *enlightened ones* are inhabiting bodies on this plane at this particular point in time. We are, indeed, entering a period of resurgence of the spiritual mode of thinking and operating. The old idea from India that when the **student** is ready, the **teacher will be there**, is true, indeed. *Teachers* have been incarnating with ever-increasing regularity since the turn of this century. They are now incarnating at a vast rate and will aid in the emerging growth that is imminent. Many of these *teachers* are coming into their own and are nearing the end of their "training" phase that was part of their game plans, and some, of advanced age, will be emerging as new psychically active entities.

This is indeed still the beginning of a new age in spirituality. Our *enlightened ones* are now able to let go of the mystical trappings of yesteryear, throwing off their robes, turbans, beads and jangling bracelets and appearing as what they are — people. The public is more sophisticated now and they do not all demand the hocus-pocus that our earlier *enlightened ones* were forced to take part in. Of course, there have always been those who pretended to be enlightened and separated many from their credulity as well as their money. What we are talking about here are the real ones: the ones who are ethical and have no wish to dupe or control others in any way. They are actually very easy to tell apart, especially these days.

As we have said before, the *enlightened ones* are people, not without their own problems since problems are an intimate part of this world. They are not supermen and superwomen who are untouched by the world, by emotions and pitfalls that beset all of humankind. They may, if anything, feel emotions more deeply due to their sensitivity — that sensitivity that makes it possible for them to be *channels* for the *spirit*.

Because people want so very much to believe that eventually, they will be without problems, troubles and worries, they insist that their *teachers* be perfect. But to insist upon that is to miss the point of being here. Such *teachers* are willing to "suffer" the consequences of life in physical form. They may at times be able to supersede some of the effects and transcend some of the pitfalls due to a greater sense of proportion and viewpoint, but they are not perfect, nor do they try to be.

These *enlightened ones* allow themselves to be used as "clear channels" and "keepers of the flame of inspiration," so to speak, and they are in constant contact with their own *spirit guides* and *teachers*. This is not an exclusive club. Anyone who is ready to look and see can become a *channel*, using direct inspiration to better their own and others' lives. The aim is to help **all** *beings* grow and expand in awareness. This is the way to win the game. The *enlightened ones* are not here to control those who haven't begun to come out of the chrysalis. They are not here to control anybody . . . only to inspire, teach and guide. They can many times lead us to acknowledgment of our own *guides* and *teachers* who have been whispering to us all this time.

The goal is to become reacquainted with your *guides* and *teachers* so that you can benefit from their guidance directly — on your own — and not be dependent upon another person to do the *channeling*. (By *channeling* we mean the conscious receiving of messages, information or concepts, feelings or even the sense of sharing moments and thoughts from another *being*, whether that other being be in or out of a body. Telepathy is a kind of *channeling*.)

Our *guides* help us keep focus on our inner knowing and on our spiritual goals. They are trying to help us "remember" our beginnings and our *Real Realities* while we are still here in *fantasy land*. They are helping us create the coming great renascence that will free humankind spiritually while regaining the connection with *All There Is*. Our games will become much richer with this conscious involvement.

In a sense, you might call the *enlightened ones spirit guides*, here in physical form, because that is basically their agreed-upon function. Since birth they have strained against the membrane of unknowing, relentlessly pushing, growing and expanding in compassion and understanding until they finally break through and are able to fulfill this function.

It is rarely easy because of the great wall of inertia that stands between humankind and spiritual awareness and freedom. It is a quest worthy of the greatest storytellers. Many times, the early lives of our *enlightened ones* are filled with great wanderings and uncertainties, various and sundry unrelated pursuits and periods of quixotic determination. Many times their thoughts and actions are bewildering to friends and family. No doubt about it, unless they are able to hide behind a social veneer and get by with it, they are considered "different" to say the least. The common denominator lies in the relentless search for enlightenment and awareness. They are individuals and they are all different from one another; and they all find the "windows" to awareness in different ways.

Some may appear to be totally disinterested in spirituality at odd times, but they always find their "center" and off they go.

If you feel that some of the above applies to you, then it is because it is true. **Everyone** will become enlightened. Some before others. But everyone will. There is no way it won't happen. But all need inspiration in order to find their way.

Each *being* who breaks through the wall of inertia weakens that wall until finally, as a species, we overcome it and our world will once again evolve and change. Only this time, we will not lose our awareness. This time we will have learned what it is to be "alone" and we will never make that mistake again.

CHAPTER TWO

GAMES

In order to better understand the part our *spirit guides* play in our lives on this plane, we need to look at the nature of the games we play here, the rules we apply and the agreements we have, not only with our *guides* but with others who are also playing games in this physical universe.

A game, for definition's sake, consists of **goals, purposes, barriers, liberties, challenges, adventure, predictable and unpredictable events, all laced with planned and unplanned details**. Occasionally, our games include opponents but mostly they don't. The anatomy of our games also includes **wins, near wins, losses and near losses**, and for our purposes it may or may not include an end result.

It is difficult for someone living in some kind of intolerable situation, experiencing the throes of terrible physical illness or financial ruin, to think of it all as a game, but that is what it is, nonetheless. Not only are they playing a game, but they are playing **their own** game. The game that they created for themselves to play.

One might say we come here to practice the use of our abilities to play a game — start one, play it through to the end and go on to the next.

Those playing games on this plane, we will call *travelers*. When we set out on our journey to this plane, we make game plans which we bring with us. They are made up of broad, sweeping goals and not planned out in detail. If they were, there would be no game.

Here are some of the examples of game goals: learning compassion, learning patience, fortitude, gathering strength and power as a *being*, experiencing deep emotion, facing dangers, creating beauty, creating havoc, forgetting and finding one's way back to remembering, reconnecting with all life everywhere, experiencing communication with old *being-friends*, recapturing old games and completing them, and we could go on and on. In other words, we come here, perfect in every way, suspend our *knowingness* and deny our *inner beingness* in order to experience the lack and then the recapturing of all those aspects listed above.

For example, there is no need to learn compassion outside the physical universe because there is no **lack** of compassion there. Get the idea? The only way we can experience separation is to come into a physical existence. The only way we can experience the blossoming of our enlightenment is to come to a world that admits the possibility of **un**enlightenment.

A part of most game plans is the enjoyment of discovering new and different points of view. Those who have been cruelly used by others will often spend great periods refusing to look at any other viewpoints, stubbornly insisting that theirs are the only ones worth having. Such *travelers* may have to play out several lifetimes before being able to shake out of old, tired and restrictive viewpoints and go on. They may experience a catastrophic event which will then shake them up enough to change or begin a change in viewpoint.

All these games and many more are played on this plane, but the main event for us all is the rediscovery of our *inner knowing*, our *inner being*, our *oneness* with all of life on every plane. It is as though we have entered the maze that makes up this existence and we set off to find our way out. That does not mean that the maze is a trap. No, it is a part of what has become the overall game of life in physical form. It also doesn't mean that the maze cannot be fun, joyful and rewarding.

It is easy when viewing life on this plane to become overly simplistic. It is not the wish here to make the physical life purposes and goals seem empty and pointless. Experience alone creates great feelings and emotions which then create greater scope, wisdom and inner strength. This adds to the vast store of all Life experience and ability, enriching the whole being. These are the goals underlying all the scenarios chosen by ourselves with which to experience Life on this plane.

Creating Our Own Demons

If we consider life here as a trap, we will no doubt project a lot of extra barriers in our own paths. We will project enemies where there are none; we will project monsters and demons; and we will become suspicious of the motives of others and even suspicious of our own, going into years and years of analysis to find the demons in our own minds.

Now, realize that if we project these demons and monsters, they do exist in our private universes and they do need to be exorcised in some way, whether it be by self-realization of truth for one's self or with the aid of another who can guide us to these realizations. We must not judge others harshly if they go for analysis or other methods for such exorcism or enlightenment, but rather, we could admire their courage to face what they think is evil in their own minds. There are many ways to search and there are many ways to find. Each person has the right to find his/her own way.

There are *beings* right here who are more than happy to personify our demons because that is the game they are here to play. These are our rapists, robbers, criminals of all sorts. They are learning what it is to be criminal and to display "evil." If they hit upon one of our projections, they are off and running to comply. Then when we have havoc played against us, we can say — "See? I told you the people in this neighborhood were no good!" There will always be those who are eager to personify our fondest wishes. It is important, then, to recognize just what it is for which we are fondly wishing.

Once we come up out of the lower reaches of the *physical universe trance state* (that state which brings into being certain limitations of our awareness so that we experience material reality as if it were the only reality), we are free from the necessity of routing our demons and free from feeling we have a lot of evil to face and conquer. Then we can start playing the game with more freedom and greater creativity.

Widely Agreed-Upon Demons

It is true that we sometimes borrow demons and evil from our environments. Families and groups to which we belong will telepathically transmit projections of one kind or another, and the whole family or group will agree upon these projections and then such projections will be "discovered" as proof of the group's beliefs.

Group fears and projected demons and witches are some examples. In Old Salem, Massachusetts, such group fears are what caused many to be pilloried or burned at the stake as witches. No doubt many of those were even convinced they **were** witches, so strong was the group-projection. The burning and castings out finally subsided because the exorcisms really worked for them.

We must be mindful of the projections we give to our children. There is no doubt that many of their fears in childhood are borrowed from those of the family and school. Telepathic pictures and concepts are unerringly projected into the child's universe at a time when it is so young that it cannot distinguish one projection from another. Many childhood nightmares mirror frightening projections of other family members. The sensitivity and strong telepathic ability of the young is such that without natural filtering that occurs later in life, the child is open and vulnerable. In an environment which is relatively free of fear and free of any strong idea of evil, a child has no need to develop filters for protection and the openness is available for fast learning and true perception.

Puberty is a time of great psychic upheaval — a time in which the old projections are taken out, looked at and discarded or kept as the case may be. It is a time of throwing off a layer of the cocoon, so to speak.

Brainwashing

"Brainwashing" is the name for conscious, premeditated and controlling projections that are done in a short, concentrated and forceful manner that can bring about complete changes in personality and viewpoints in days or weeks, sometimes hours. Such programs or practices are most effective at times in one's life in which old projections are beginning to fade, due mostly to lack of constant reinforcement. They can come at any time in life because each individual has his own experience. But definitely, puberty is the most traumatic season of change that we are ever likely to face. The groupthink is so strong at this time due to the power released from the psyche that the world literally rocks with the force of it. Whole changes in our world have been wrought by such power of projections. These projections can be so powerful and so very different that they are viewed as truth. Exciting and demanding truth. Most of them have enough truth in them that they gather quickly those who are really ready for change.

There are occasions in which one succumbs to "brainwashing" as a means of survival only, such as prisoners of war sometimes face. One becomes convinced that he can even save his buddies in this way.

Although we are all responsible for our state of existence at any given time, there are situations in which we become overwhelmed and are more easily influenced. The point of overwhelm is different for each individual and we must have compassion for those who cannot resist.

At this point, let us go back and pick up the threads of our "game."

Stages of the Game

1. We decide to enter this plane.
2. Before doing so, we lay out general plans for the types of games we will be playing.
3. We share these plans with our chosen *spirit guides*.
4. We then come and take on physical form.
5. We learn by observing and by telepathic projection. At the beginning we are not equipped to make value judgments on these projections, so we accept them all, in whatever manner we can until we can think for ourselves.
6. At puberty, these projections begin to fall apart and the confusion leaves us ripe for new ones.
7. The next big change is going out on our own. Life and values are changed by the sheer realities of survival. New attitudes form and goals may change or take new turns at this point. Due to the nature of our goals, there are many different kinds of games we can play that will satisfy these goals. We may try different games and views at different times in our lives in order to broaden our spectrum of experience. We will often put ourselves into a totally foreign situation in order to learn from it or enjoy the excitement of it.
8. The next change comes either through location, losing one's job or changing jobs. Perhaps the loss of a close friend or family member comes at this time. This change is due mainly to relationships and changes surrounding relationships. Accidents or illness resulting in physical impairment may also be a part of

the change here.

9. There are other changes which may or may not occur at this point. Perhaps a period of disillusionment, followed by a new look at old goals. Heavy business losses or gains. Catastrophies of weather phenomena or fire. A growing concern over aging without having fulfilled life goals or one's own potential. Separation and divorce or career change may occur at this juncture in an effort to renew one's interest in life and the future.

Finally we reach a point at which we feel we **must** make changes. We can no longer tolerate life as it is. We may feel trapped or wound tightly into a mold that is no longer comfortable. We have been changing and growing all along but finally the gulf between "then and now" becomes so wide that we must break out.

If we are married with children, we may blame them for our feelings. Such is not the case, but many families have broken apart for this reason. If the marriage partner is willing to grow and change as well, both lives can be served equally at this juncture. If not, then separation is inevitable. A *being* will many times set aside his or her own desires for growth and change to satisfy promises made, but life will not be happy or fruitful for either party.

It is not our intention here to state the wrongness or rightness of broken marriages. We are merely describing a very real problem that cannot be ignored. There are probably as many patterns of growth cycles as there are *beings* who are experiencing them.

Growth brings about a greater understanding and responsibility, so it cannot justify heartlessly casting aside those we have loved and who have loved and cared for us. The manner in which we affect these life-changes is indicative of the level of our growth. Depending upon the length of life, No. 9 can occur more than once with each new change bringing about a new beginning.

10. There follows here a period of introspection, whether on a level of ready awareness or in the sleep state. It can also occur on a level just beneath awareness. This period could be called the *floating period* and can occur at more than one time in life. It could even last throughout an entire life experience, coincidentally with all the other periods of life.

This is the time in which the *being* begins to awaken to *Real Reality* outside this dimension. We could actually take all these periods and stretch them out to encompass the different **kinds** of games we play, one lifetime to another. For example: One's first life on this plane could very well follow the trail of childhood — a vulnerable kind of life, becoming oriented to this world and its symbols — then a lifetime full of the turmoil of puberty. Perhaps this is the life that one might wish to try criminality as a game or perhaps other kinds of attitudes that present themselves during puberty. A time of great power and energy, growth and motion. Get the idea? So that at each juncture of development as a *being* we could experience many possible types of outlet, depending upon our game plans.

We can readily see that if we choose a life partner who is playing games as one who is approaching life from the viewpoint of pubescent games and we are in the lifetime that includes the period of introspection, the relationship will be difficult. We will feel lonely for someone who can share with our own feelings as we awaken. They will feel lonely for someone who can play their games with them. And we would all be right. For there is no wrong way to live. All life is perfect for its purpose and for the purpose of all life.

11. The next most volatile period of change comes about in "old age." Some of the most exciting changes of one's life can occur at this time. Those who die young do not get to experience it. Some of the elderly think they are senile or going insane because of the power of these psychic emanations that turn life upside down. Many are living alone at this age and those around them do not understand what is happening either, so the elderly get bypassed due to the almost total lack of insight into this period of life.

People who are older than the mainstream of humanity are looked upon as more stupid than those who are running about, having careers, making money, heading corporations and raising families. As a species, we tend to downgrade those whom we do not understand, and we understand less about aging than any other period in life.

There are other societies which treat the elderly with more respect, but they do not understand these emanations either. Their projections and feelings of responsibility are broad enough to include the care of their older family members, however.

The phenomena of old-age awakening can come also to one who is nearing the end of physical life. A certain amount of pragmatism and resignation mixed with other periods of almost childlike enjoyments and discoveries are all a part of this period. Many who are called "senile" are merely beginning to waft in and out of dimensions much as they did in babyhood or early childhood. With age comes the ability to consider alternate frameworks of understanding. There is fear at this stage because no one else seems to understand, not even others experiencing the same phenomena. So ideas of this sort are rarely even shared with those of similar age. Most are afraid of being placed in mental and physical prisons as a reward for long life, so they run away as far as possible from growing realizations.

Many times this attitude results in bitterness and "negative" personality changes which make them hard to get along with.

For those who began to blossom earlier in life, there is comfort in knowing what is happening. The joy inherent in the natural opening-up process during advanced body age makes for much enrichment and happiness.

There should be classes to help those who are going through such changes. They should be helped to understand what is happening to and for them.

12. After body death, we enter into a special period of reorientation to the *spirit world*. In truth, we are always residing in the *spirit world* even while living life in physical form. There are differences, however, in our focus so we need to reorient. If we have strong expectations surrounding "life after death," then we tend to project those. Our *spirit guides* help us through this period much as a mother whale helps her baby until it can surface for breath. They may even join in the fun of our theatrics and live out a short time of our "life after death scenario," playing the parts of various personages we expect to meet "on the other side." Very soon, however, with their gentle coaching, we begin to recall the *Real Realities* and rejoin our *spirit friends* and *families* with full recall.

13. The next period is usually one spent in looking back at the life just led — considering the game played — deciding whether or not one has gained all that was hoped for or planned for. There are three ways in which we evaluate our lives on this plane and they have nothing to do with the measure of success or failure in societal terms:

   1) The depth to which we were willing to experience Life. How thoroughly did we dip into our emotions and experiences?
   2) The grace with which we came out of the experience. (Persistence is a part of this.)
   3) What we were able to garner as a result of the experience. The reward in terms of spiritual growth and expansion.

This is all by which we measure ourselves.

After a period of rest and renewed joy, one may decide upon a new game to play in this physical universe. The time spent in between could be years or even centuries of Earth time. New game plans will be devised and shared — new or old *spirit guides* will be "chosen" for the new body experience. New parents and situations will be chosen, and off we go again.

It has been observed that many times a baby is born with great troubles, cries a lot, is angry much of the time or demanding. These babies sometimes grow up and never change, continuing to have great problems as well as being a great problem to everyone. One explanation for this is the fact that a *being* does not choose to engage in a period of reorientation, reflection and rest, and comes almost directly back into physical existence. No real plan is shared with *guides* — no real future plans are made and life begins with catch as catch can. Also, all the problems of the just-past life which weren't resolved in that life are still fresh and alive and the new beginning is choppy and not well organized. Such a fast reentry is usually made by the unaware who are convinced that this world is all there is and it may take many lifetimes to come up and out of that circuit.

Children who are experiencing this, need special understanding, quiet and calm environmental climate in which to "cool down," so to speak. Their condition is mostly one of overstimulation and they literally need a vacation. The one they didn't take between lives. It is not easy for the parents of such a child, but much future anguish can be avoided if a calm, serene and very quiet atmosphere can be provided. Loud voices, loud noises and other kinds of excitement can set off a whole week of crying and demanding of constant attention. Baby sitters must be quiet types — unexcitable and stable.

It can be fully understood that a parent is not totally responsible for how a child develops. One *being* can only do so much for another. The rest is up to each individual.

Other Cultures

There are some societies in which the growth and development trail is different from what has been described here. Tribes in Africa, South America, Australia and in spots all over the globe are close-knit and leave little room for change of any kind that is significant. Some groups have changed with the introduction of Western influences and they are going through a kind of puberty as a society.

Their belief systems have been so ingrained and handed down with little or no alteration that even if the symbols have lost their spontaneity, they are adhered to without question so the ancient projections are constantly being reinforced. Eventually, an iconoclast or two will enter the fold and give trouble but they are inevitably cast out to keep the group pure. Many times all are told that they will forever reincarnate into the same tribe. They do, so the projections are kept constantly refreshed, a continuous re-creation.

In countries which are totally male dominated, we can find some differences in growth cycles, but these will have definite similarities to what we have cited here.

To some extent, each country and society perpetuates itself much in the same manner as the African tribe, with changes being accomplished very slowly.

Almost unerringly, these remote tribes of people, in whatever country they appear, are aware of other universes and altered states of consciousness. They have very sophisticated methods of casting out demons when they appear. These groups have "medical" treatments using vibrations in the form of music or noisemakers that can indeed effect "cures." They have learned very effective uses of herbs and other earth elements to effect healing. The facts that their beliefs are not written up in slick-paper volumes with leather bindings, and their healing instruments are not kept in stainless steel cabinets in an antiseptic state do not mean that they do not work. They very probably wouldn't work with someone from the West because the belief-systems are too different. One would have to completely suspend one's beliefs in order to allow the treatment to do its job. In like manner, if we expect them to benefit from any of our Western methods, we need to help them in some way to suspend their beliefs long enough to let our methods work.

There are many people living in the Western world today who cannot get better with modern medicine because they have lost faith in it and can no longer agree upon the telepathic message that says, "This will make it all better."

People in remote societies are also playing the game of life on this plane and they are learning too. They **decided** to play the game on those playing fields just as you have decided yours. It is true that due to the strong agreement and command that they reincarnate within the same group or unit, they become ingrown. To that degree they may be living whole lives of relative unproductiveness as regards spiritual growth. We find the same thing happening in all societies.

Outside Influences

With the introduction of even one new element from the outside world, the possibilities of new growth and change become limitless again. The whole structure does not need to be changed in order for a complete transformation to eventually occur. Much as in biocultures in laboratory experiments, changes introduced into the environment enter an almost infinite number of variables possible in the existing structure.

The changes are not always seen as positive. Heretofore peaceful, tribes can turn into marauders. Anarchistic groups within the society's structure may spring up, causing havoc and upset in the entire spiritual as well as physical environments. Such environments may have remained relatively unchanged perhaps for centuries.

These upheavals can be short- or long-term, can be the cause of new, more growth-inspiring communities or even be the vehicle by which the community will break apart and disperse to exist as a unit no more.

It is not always a good thing to send zealous souls into a long-term and firmly established, well-running, happy and peaceful society with the aim of totally changing the entire structure to fit another society's idea of how everyone here must play the game of life. To infer or otherwise state that an entire group of people who have been surviving and growing are somehow inferior and must cast aside all they have depended upon for centuries as stable points of reference, is to ring the death knell on the rights of that society and on the individuals within it.

Connection made between societies is just as important as connection made between different worlds and realities. These connections allow us to expand our *knowingness* and the scope of our growth. Many times we find that an idea different from ideas we have held for long periods of time may serve to open up whole vistas that were hidden to us. Reaching out to other points of view and other realities is always rewarding. It may also be disturbing or even upsetting. This is a normal reaction. After all, changing one's viewpoints can be unsettling and confusing until one has refocused. It is all a part of reconnecting with other parts of *All There Is*.

Self-Imposed Barriers

Not every *being* is on the same rung of the growth-ladder, and the games will differ in length and intensity. The more advanced *beings* will often lay out a game with great barriers to overcome. The greater the barrier, the greater the reward. Now, remember, the reward need not be actualized on this plane in order to satisfy the rule of the original game.

Watching others, it may seem obvious just what kinds of games they are playing. This kind of evaluation can be highly inaccurate because the **details** of a game may actually mask the real game being played and may have little to do with the reward that is being sought. We do better when we evaluate our own games and play them as best we can. Leave others to find and further their own games unless they ask for aid. Any aid must be given with the understanding that we can give a helping hand without trying to play the game for someone else. Our aid, then, should be minimal, leaving the other *being* more able to see things for himself. In this way we are returning power to the *being* rather than taking it away by doing too much, and this is the way our *guides* like to help us. They never take away our power — even our power to choose against their advices.

Total Acceptance

We have all searched for "our people," those who accept us instantly as ourselves and understand instantly who we are and expect nothing else from us than being ourselves. We have all looked for the closeness that we experience with our *spirit families*, who really do accept and understand us as we are. (*Spirit families* are those large groups of *beings* with whom we have spent most of eternity. They are beings who have been drawn together by similar goals and viewpoints. It is from these *families* that our *spirit guides* are chosen.)

Due to the fact that everybody on this plane is busy playing their own games, it is difficult for one person to be "all" to the other. For us to expect that of another is to actually be unwilling for the one we love to play his or her own game. There may be the rare *being* whose game is to help someone else play theirs. There is a great chance that such a partnership can become very boring.

This life here is not easy, and the best we can do is find some wonderfully interesting person who feels as we do about life and then set about helping each other live life as productively and happily as possible.

We, on the other hand, are not here to be "all" for anyone else. What we have actually been searching for are our *spirit guides* and *spirit families*. When we are reunited with them, our relationships can and will be more comfortable on this plane and we can more easily recognize another as a fellow *traveler*. We can stop expecting other *travelers* to be our *spirit guides*.

We Are Not Here to Play Someone Else's Game

It is not only impossible but nonoptimal for one *being* to try to be "all" for another, because the price of that is the subjugation of one's own game and growth potential. It is also not good for the one who is being catered to. We never win, truly, when we use another in order to do so. The best we can do is find those of similar ideas and growth so that our games are more comfortable and our growth more in tune with our own thrusts and not through trying to usurp the energies of another in order to carry us through.

There are those who are looking for someone to help them play out a part or parts of their own games, and perhaps one game goes counter to the other. We must recognize when this happens so we can avoid entanglements that will hold us back. We will sometimes get involved with one who needs to climb over us in order to satisfy a **detail** in his own game, with no thought of our rights as *travelers*. We may even recognize it when we are doing the same thing.

There are two things working here: One, is that one is so unaware of the real nature of life here that he cannot recognize that others are also trying to satisfy their own game plans. They may even think that money is all that is necessary to secure the unfailing devotion of another.

Two, is that those who go along with such a person are probably equally unaware of the real nature of life here and may be suffering from a case of unworthiness and actually seem to need subjugation to satisfy that belief. The fact that there are no victims also applies here. However, for one to be overbearing of another, no matter what the reason, is not optimum. To justify and say, oh, well, she would have found someone else to cater to, is a gross misjudgment of the facts. To recognize that someone is searching for suppression and then to provide that suppression is using it as a justification **not** to help the other, not to return power to the other, but to satisfy a need to suppress... Get the idea? Neither viewpoint contains growth or understanding.

There could be a third reason. One player may simply be returning a favor or debt from another life or existence and, when the favor has been paid, will wish to continue as before. However, and this is a very big **however**, no debt owed can ever really be cleanly paid back at the expense of either party, but must be paid easily and lovingly. In truth, such "debts" are not real and exist only in the mind. Only if one thinks there is a debt, does it exist at all.

What if we see situations such as one or two above? Shouldn't we interfere and try to set things straight? Yes, but in the most minimum ways possible. We must resist the temptation to **save** people from themselves. Only if we can clearly see that the scale remains tipped on one side for far too long, with too much damage or overwhelm occurring on one side, should we attempt to give more than a gentle helping hand. And even then, the persons involved must be given a chance to **reach** for that helping hand.

The thrust we feel in wanting to help is very real and we do feel compassion for our friends. We must take great care, however, in **how** we help and in how much. Many times, these extreme experiences serve as catalysts. They stir up the "compost heap," so to speak, letting in air and making room for more growth. The more we become aware, the more we can recognize the direction our involvements are taking us and decide at the beginning whether it is something we are willing to experience or not.

In trying to get it all straight in our minds, there is also the danger of becoming too suspicious of one another. It is really quite all right to help someone play out a part of a game as long as we are also able to advance on the game board. Indeed, there are times we are greatly advanced by the act of loving and selfless help itself. There is a point at which the tide turns, however, and it is not healthy for either game for one to do all the helping. Both games are slowed and perhaps even stopped during such a period.

It is not up to us to decide when another *being* needs change. Each *traveler* will decide when she/he is tired of a condition. That is not to say we can't plant a seed or make gentle suggestions or even offer a hand up. Much more than that is likely to create greater refusal and determination not to budge. We, on the other hand, do not have to sacrifice our own games in order to stick around waiting for the other to change. We too can get tired of our lack of self-determination and move on to more productive fields.

It is important, especially after regaining awareness of the anatomy of games on this plane, to orchestrate and choreograph our existences to accommodate our own growth while allowing the growth of others. It is hard to grow around those who refuse to grow or who are growing in different directions. We must recognize their rights to their own lives as well as our rights to the **speed** at which we wish to advance during any given period.

We could also look at the fact that experiencing the lower reaches of this universe is one of our reasons for coming, and if we are ready to rise up out of them, it is only because we have satisfied our own curiosities about those lower reaches and have gained what we came here to gain. Now, isn't it silly to condemn someone else who has not yet satisfied those curiosities and is not ready to rise up out of those lower reaches? How soon we forget our own histories.

The more objective we can be in relation to the games of others, the easier it is for us to move in and around the environments of other *travelers* who feel as we do or at least who are ready for new spurts of growth. We can be very exciting for each other during these times.

It is not unkind to leave someone or a group to find their own way, so long as we are convinced that our help is not accomplishing anything for either of us. Our departure may well even be just that thing needed to help the other *traveler* burst loose. We cannot, however, be the judge of another's game, of speed of growth or of nongrowth. Even a *being* living as a rock or tree is experiencing some kind of growth.

In fact, **everything** we do is a part of growing. There is no other game. Everything we do is spiritual, no matter how it seems.

Viewpoints on Help

To the degree we satisfy our original game plans, to that same degree we grow and expand. Therein lies the secret to growth and expansion as *beings*. Another part of the secret may very well be our willingness to aid others in their quests. Perhaps even a smile at the right time can have a great deal to do with what happens in another's personal world. Sometimes, to acknowledge another's existence is to acknowledge our own. There are many ways in which we can be of help to others. Doing it **all** for them is certainly not one of the ways. That is no help at all, no matter how it appears. That is manipulation.

We find those who want it both ways...to have all problems solved and expand as independent agents at the same time. This is a situation in which one does not permit the other. One cannot be dependent upon someone else to solve all one's problems or even most of one's problems and then expect to grow in enlightenment. It just doesn't work that way.

This is not to say that if we find someone hanging from a cliff, we stand and talk and tell him just how powerful he is and tell him all about how he can climb up by himself. That first helping hand, lifting one up from an abyss, can be the best way to help sometimes. But to go further and further, separating one from his own self-determination and power, is to carry help too far. We do this over and over again and then wonder why others do not appreciate all our "help." Our *spirit guides* know this and they know it well. They use it in relation to us. They never help us so much that they, not we, are playing our games.

There is another concept here, regarding help. As we grow in awareness, our compassion takes on deeper tones, rich and full; and when we see others in trouble, hungry, in apathy, afraid, we feel it intensely. To withhold our help is near to impossible. To feel deeply about anything and not be able to express it is painful. That is because we are all essentially loving and generous.

Those needing our help are there for us to see. They are there for us to experience the high, heady feeling of having helped in a meaningful way. The world hunger, the millions of homeless, desolate and lost friends — all *beings* who are a part of us — are giving us the opportunity to view a need and do something about fulfilling that need.

So, you can see that we are not all just islands in a stream of consciousness with only our own games going forward, but we are here to view the lives of others and we are here providing a life for others to view.

> In order for this world to fulfill itself, we must interact together, forming a full circle of reality — a great ballet of spirit and experience, choreographed perfectly to afford each of us a starring role in the game of *Life*.

Other Game Plans

A game might simply be to search for and find as many different viewpoints as possible and by these viewpoints enrich the life of the *traveler* and even aid the *traveler* in finding his way back *home*, carrying riches of spirit and personal growth.

Another game might be to play games on this plane, putting so many barriers there that one can't discover one's way back or even know that there **is** a way back at all for a very long time — perhaps even hundreds of lifetimes. It can easily be seen that the end results of our games may not be at all related to the success or failure of the smaller games we play as a part of the societies and times in which we live.

There are also other goals which may be connected to the period or age in which you are living at this time. It is no coincidence that certain *beings* incarnate or reincarnate at certain times. Sometimes, whole groups have previously agreed to come together for various reasons. In every age can be traced groups (not always working together knowingly, but intertwined through similarity of actions) which have common ideas. Sometimes whole groups find themselves drawn together lifetime after lifetime by similar interests.

For instance, types of inventions, art, books, philosophies, tend to come together in bunches. This is an age of "high-tech" scientific urges and drives, and at the same time there is a greater surge along spiritual lines than has appeared for a very long time. It is obvious that certain groups are working together on these goals and purposes. It is no accident that many with similar game plans have incarnated at the same time.

Now, no matter how it looks sometimes, we **do** overcome all the obstacles and we make "game points" on the **ways** in which we overcome them. These **ways** may not always pass a society's standard on what constitutes winning or losing. In fact, in many instances, what might be viewed as failure on this plane could very well translate as total victory in retrospect when being viewed outside this world and its criteria.

Our entire experience here on this plane consists of a series of learnings and translations, adventures and misadventures, all pushed through the sieve of this-world symbols.

Laughter

One truth about *beings* is that when we decide to take something seriously (such as this universe), we go all the way and do we ever take it **seriously**! Laughter helps to break down the solidity of this existence and its symbols, and sometimes we are afraid everything will disappear altogether if we are too humorous or have too much fun. There are worlds that do disappear when there is much laughter, but these worlds follow different laws of cause and effect. Our world will definitely respond to laughter by making heavy emotions disappear, but not objects. Objects may take on lighter significances, however, through laughter.

The more seriously we take our game, the harder it is to realize our goals. It takes a sense of humor to come out freely on the other side. It is even possible that the more seriously we take our game, the longer it takes to play it out and may even take several lifetimes to fulfill one game we have set out for ourselves.

The Sleep State and Dreams

During our sleep and reverie times we venture beyond set symbols and consider life in quite a different manner. We have trouble remembering from one frame of reference to the other, so we cloak our dreams and reveries in physical universe clothes. The trouble with that is that the clothes don't fit and the translations suffer greatly, leaving us with only a distorted picture of the experience. We are sometimes aware that certain problems seem to have resolved themselves by morning, making things clear and understandable. At such times we are actually working out our problems, trying to put the pieces together and we often do, while the body sleeps. The more we learn to be "conscious" during the sleep experience, the more we can benefit from answers we can find there. We relate to *Earth symbols* in a highly selective and individual sense over and above any collective agreement. Because of this, it is very difficult, if not impossible, for another person to decipher the exact meanings of our dreams for us. It is something we need to learn for ourselves.

Our *spirit guides* are here to help us with such translations and to help us bridge the gap between this world and the rest of life which includes all dimensions and all other worlds. In fact — *All There Is*.

Life and Relationships Are Not Always Easy

Now, realize that when we talk of games, we are not negating the fact that life here is hard and we are not telling you that it is all a kid's game and you are merely going through the motions, tripping about giddily, not knowing where you are going, living out life without meaning or purpose. **Not at all**. We do realize that it is not easy to live out life here, trying to survive in a body that hurts easily and must be fed, clothed and rested. At the same time one can learn how to get along with others who are having the same or similar problems.

Relationships can be difficult at the best of times. We can learn how to perpetuate the good feelings we have about one another while still maintaining our own self-determination and our own goals. We can learn, somehow, to do all this and still remain friends and lovers. No, it is not easy.

There are so many different avenues to life that must be dealt with — so many viewpoints to consider and at the same time progress on our own game boards. You are to be congratulated for being willing to play a game here at all. Your rewards are great, however, and those rewards are the real reason you are here. To gain for yourself the kind of understanding that can only be gained in a world such as this one is of a very high order and you must never feel you are a pawn in some great unknowable cosmic game. You will consciously be able to view your life's game here when you are finished with it, and you will consciously be able to evaluate it and congratulate yourself for doing very well, indeed, in the face of all the barriers and stresses and fears of not being able to "make it."

The Changes in Games and Viewpoints

With growth and enlightenment, it is possible to realize what you have gained while still here, enriching your life even more. It is all in the assumption of a viewpoint.

As we have outlined earlier, there are many times during a life in which our directions can change. At times, we resist these changes and they may be postponed for a while, but eventually, with help, we are able to make even drastic turns in our lives and take on whole new viewpoints, endeavors and even new sets of friends. There are games within games. Smaller games can enrich the whole. In looking back, you can see the times in which you were either playing games within games or going through vast changes that would alter the entire course of your life. This may have happened a number of times. Depending upon the goals, a *being* may or may not take advantage of these probable or possible states of change. But all of us contemplate them all the same.

Contrary to the idea that life is meant for the pursuit of happiness and monetary and societal success, all with grand and glorious endings — we would like to have you look at *Reality*. We come here to **experience**, not to avoid or run away from the lower depths of this universe. We came here to experience it all and from one lifetime to another we do, in fact, experience everything we came for.

Sometimes, even in a divorce, the stress and pain of separation is all a part of shaking us loose from a nonproductive period and we need the change in order to attain a new spurt of personal growth.

The converse is also true, that sometimes when we are able to salvage a relationship, both partners will emerge renewed and able to take on more viewpoints, thus furthering their individual and collective games.

Now, understanding that there are no victims, we can see that we have all agreed to suffer the consequences that are inherent in our games. And **all** games have consequences. They are part of the anatomy of growth and experience.

Giving, Receiving and Balance

One trap that *beings* seem to fall into in this dimension is the belief that everything has to balance. If there is good, there must also be evil. If there is happiness, there must be sadness. If there is health, there must be illness. And if there is good luck, it must follow that there is bad luck and usually just after.

People have been known to say, "Everything is going too well" or "This is much too easy, something bad is sure to happen." **Not so!!!!** These conditions occur only when we lay these on our tracks. Whatever we lay on the tracks ahead of us is what we get. More about this point later.

If we had really wanted a trouble-free existence, we would not have come here at all. It is not that these consequences are preordained, but they do follow laws of this universe. Those laws are only partially understood at this time. These are very intricate laws that flow in and around all the games that are played in any given dimension or part of a dimension (our planet is a part of this third dimension).

Imagine the multiplicity of games that are being played even on one block of one street in any given city. Then imagine the myriad of games that are being played on this planet. The flows that interchange and admit the existence of each game are wondrous things. We simply could not exist here without each other's help and willingness to play roles.

So we **can** give without **having** to receive. Isn't that a relief? When we give, however, we do receive energies for ourselves, so it isn't a total loss. But if we live out life making sure that there is a receipt for everything given, we will lose the ability to give freely and honestly. What a loss! Giving is what *beings* do best.

There are those who cannot give and they appear to take and take. But that is because they do not understand that they are full and need to give in order to empty the font of givingness, therefore becoming able to really receive more. They fancy they are empty and must be filled by others because they think they cannot **give** gifts to themselves — of love, laughter and caring and nurturing, so they feel they have to take it from others. It can be uncomfortable to others because more than physical-universe objects must satisfy this apparent emptiness, and the *being* will try to drain energies from others. And the others really do **feel** drained. One feels drained only when the giving is forced from them at their partial unwillingness.

Now, while energies are limitless and never used up, one does feel as though something more than one was willing to give has been taken. Because, on this plane, we have agreed to limits; we limit our own energies and in that context it is possible to drain us of them. Simply stop agreeing to let yourself be so drained and it will stop. It is not good for either party — whether receiving, taking or giving of energies in this manner. Draw upon the universal energies that are available to you and all others. Help those who feel empty to start flowing **out** so they can again be filled with their own life-giving power and energy.

Purposes

Now, while the **details** of our games do not reflect our purposes here on this plane, the manner in which we play our games does. That is not to say that there are moral judgments placed upon the way we choose to play our games. What is meant here is simply our willingness to allow recognition of *All There Is* to occur. Within that recognition lies the quality of our games and the lightness with which we play them.

While our purposes may seem to be the helping of others, we can first understand the part our own growth plays in those purposes. We cannot expect to be immune from the sufferings, pressures and lessons that this world affords just because we chase around saving everyone from evil and from themselves. We can take stock and realize that we are here to play the game of life on this plane, once we are here. There are those who seem to be able to waft back and forth between dimensions and relate to each on its terms, but these are rare and unusual *beingnesses* who have ceased reincarnating through any need for the growth experience.

We Are Here to Experience, Not to Judge

Our games reflect the extent of our curiosities and no game is "better" than another. We experience those aspects of this universe that most satisfy our own curiosities. The lower reaches of this dimension are fulfilling in their own ways and we cannot be judged by our involvement in them.

If we were to step into the personal universes of others, we could see that each one has a basic purpose and the attaining of that purpose is as well-directed and important as any purpose of nobility or greatness that may be expressed and attained by anyone. Each individual is doing the best he or she can do in any given situation or scenario, and the attaining of goals through our games is the basis of all our games.

CHAPTER THREE

HOW WE RELATE TO THIS UNIVERSE

We are each a part of *All There Is* and that includes all dimensions, all *beingnesses*, all of *Life* in the vast everywhere. Separateness, however, is a this-world invention. Imagine the most individual of individuals who is yet an integral and intimate part of everything and everyone and that comes close to an accurate description of the potentialities that individuals have on this plane.

It is true that while living in and relating to this universe, we can also be fully aware of other dimensions, other *beingnesses* who live in and around it or who choose to communicate to us here on a telepathic level. We can even be aware of *beingnesses* who are not aware of us, such as ghosts or others seemingly trapped between worlds. We can be aware of the *fairy world* or *plane*. We can be aware of anything of which we allow ourselves to become aware. We would have to go beyond the farthest reaches of our imaginations to come up with something that is not already true. That is how aware we are of *All There Is*.

We are all as much involved in what is happening everywhere as we are involved with our intimate surroundings and happenings. Our very natures are multidimensional and not limited by space, time, matter or energy. We are, in a sense, visitors to this universe. We are interdimensional *travelers* who take on physical form in order to experience physical existence. This does not necessarily limit our awareness of other existences.

Sleep, Time and Other Universes

Certainly, when our bodies sleep, we take flight into other worlds, living more than one life at a "time." But then, since time is relative only to a physical plane, it stretches and bends and folds in upon itself, depending upon the laws of any given physical universe. In a less solid universe, time is also less structured and may even manifest itself in different ways at different junctures.

For instance, there is a physical universe much more conducive to fun and games than is the one you inhabit. Time is molded to fit the occasion. It lengthens for long vacations and shortens for quick trips. It lengthens when great celebrations occur or when one wants to savor a phenomenon, much as we would love to have a sunset last longer. Time can be folded upon itself so that many more experiences can take place at the same "time." That particular universe is a great favorite among *beings*.

Time is not the only thing that can be manipulated, but also color, sound, and tactile and emotional experiences can be enhanced and manipulated.

Learning how to manipulate that world is all a part of the reasons for being there. It is often the sole reason for one's visit there at all.

Manipulation of Our Universe

Let's look back to our world which is a segment of an entire physical universe in which there are also possibilities of manipulating matter, energy, space and time. The results of such manipulations are much more subtle, therefore much more precious and harder to accomplish.

Artists are constantly manipulating portions of this universe in order to create the effect they wish to create. No one could manipulate color (with the use of oils) to actually contain light, life and motion as did Vincent van Gogh. One can copy these paintings, but the natural genius that fired Vincent to paint as he did would be missing.

There are few who have ever been able to play Lizst's piano compositions with the same life, genius, fire and emotion as he himself. The same could be said of Paganini, the violinist who loved to show off — playing entire violin concertos with one or two strings. Even he did not understand or fully appreciate what he was doing.

The artist Paul Klee was able to incorporate various facets of interdimensionality that remain alive even in imperfect prints. There are conceptual communications beneath the outer layers of his paintings that draw one in with the promise of knowledge and fulfillment. The longer one looks at his paintings, the more one sees or understands, even if subliminally. At times the paintings can elicit deep emotion, depending upon the viewer. At the very least they remain enigmatic representations of the depth of feeling and perception that were an intrinsic part of Klee the artist and Klee the *being*.

We could go on citing one artist after another and how they manipulated this world in such a way as to bring out our interdimensionality which is a part of our natural heritage.

As we learn to manipulate time, we are surprised when it works. On a trip, for instance, how many times do we have "blank spots" in which we seemingly "forget" various stages of the journey. "How did I get from there to here?" we ask. At these times we are manipulating matter, energy, space and time. There are many instances in which we do this and never recognize that we have done it.

Recall the statement — "Time passes fast when I'm having fun." We can stretch time as well. Have you ever arrived at a destination fully intending to be on time, but knowing there isn't enough "time," yet you arrive not only on time, but slightly early? You have stretched time. Even if you are only slightly late, you still stretched time and made it "somehow."

Many times we seem to be only able to manipulate time, space matter or energy when the necessity is strong — the child who "somehow" finds the strength to pull an adult from a fire...someone lifting a heavy object that would ordinarily be "impossible" to lift...finding just the perfect handhold that enables one to climb back up from the face of a cliff...discovering a hitherto unknown opening in a cave in which one is lost...finding water in a desert. All these are examples of manipulation of the elements that make up this world. We consider such events to be coincidental or accidental. What they are, are natural abilities unleashed by the power of intention brought on by necessity.

The "raw materials" of this world were created by the *Creator*, but we use these raw materials to create the world that we know. This world is a by-product of our desire as individuals to be creative and to play games together and to express ourselves in ways other than ethereal. But that which is truly **real**, lies **outside** the confines of matter, energy, space and time as we understand it. We often refer to that which is truly real as the *Real Reality*.

Out of the Body Experiences
and Recognizing Real Reality

This physical universe reality is reached through a *deep trance state* in which *Real Reality* is temporarily suspended. What we experience when we have out-of-body episodes is not necessarily *Real Reality*. If we are out of the body but viewing, relating and responding to the physical universe exclusively, then we are only slightly removed from our ordinary, everyday state. We are simply viewing the physical universe from a slightly different angle. It is, however, a lovely state and much happier than our usual states. From this state we can reach further out and contact higher states. We can also contact higher states without experiencing vivid out-of-body states by looking inward into our inner selves, but that is taken up in a later chapter.

Now, if we are experiencing out-of-body episodes, flying around and enjoying this universe, it stands to reason that we are still in it, still in a *physical universe trance state*. In order to relate to and view the physical universe, we have to be in that state. This does not in any way decrease the beauty of the out-of-body state. It is a high physical universe state, but is not the *astral plane*. It is a lower harmonic or echo of the *astral plane*. It is the state in which we share some reality with ghosts, poltergeists and projections. The only difference between us and them is that we can relate to the physical universe on more than one level. We can return to our bodies when we wish; we can exercise great mobility and we are not repeating a *death experience* over and over.

The reality of this state is simply that we are out of the body without having to experience bodily death, and we can return to the body at will.

The out-of-body state is not the state that carries us **out** of the physical universe. *Real Reality* dwells **within**, not without. Higher states are discovered within ourselves, not within the physical universe.

Picture a fly at the window, trying to get out. He butts his body against the window pane over and over again, never thinking to go the other way. He thinks he sees freedom there. He will continue to try getting out through the window until he dies. We do that sometimes, butt our heads against a window only to find it is a blind alley and does not lead us where we want to go. We may, however, be able to **see** our freedom from that viewpoint, and therein lies the beauty — just as the fly can "see" freedom beyond the window pane but has not yet learned how to reach it.

The higher *physical universe trance state* coupled with higher psychic or "toward *Real Reality*" states are the tools for building Heaven right here on earth with the freedom to move around without the body and to project ourselves anywhere we want to go, unhampered — then with *knowingness* having awakened us to our *inner beingness*, we can create a world here that is so stunning and beautiful that we will realize why it was we really came.

Now, experiencing out-of-body states by itself is not enough to bring enlightenment any more than swimming under water is. There are other ways in which *beings* can go. There are the ones who go further into the physical universe and its symbols — making great significance out of physical signs. They go into deep mysticisms, delving into deeper and deeper significances. In coming out of the physical universe we find less and less significance and far fewer hidden meanings in symbols and physical objects.

Imagine the experience of being out of the body and at the same time aware of other dimensions, *inner beingness*, the inner beingness of others, the God and Christ within, the connection with *All There Is* and the feeling of intense joy that all this would bring about — and you can see somewhat the potentials of life here on this plane. We would then be living here, but again be connecting with *Real Reality*. We can, however, experience other dimensions without ever having "out-of-body" episodes, i.e., seeing the physical universe while being exterior to the body.

When we go into deep, altered states and find great joy, release and peace, and at the same time understand more about the physical universe, then we are experiencing *Real Reality*. Now, understand that in *Real Reality* we can also perceive what could be judged as negative forces, pictures and projections by self and others. From the viewpoint of this physical realm we could misassess what we see and not realize we are tapped into *Real Reality*. This happens in our dream state all the time. When our sleep experiences are translated to correspond with physical universe symbols, we sometimes fancy fearful and quite exotic realities which if truly translated would seem usual — even familiar.

If you walked down the street and met a person with purple skin, the first inclination would be to wonder what kind of malady would cause such a thing to happen. One would most certainly think there was something "wrong." The ordinary person would have an awful time dealing with the possibility that purple skin is a normal color on another planet and that perhaps, indeed, just such a person is standing there on the street. There would also be those who wouldn't even see the purple person because their belief systems would not even admit such a possibility at all.

Getting used to the idea that one will come upon phenomena that are so different from anything hitherto experienced in this life will assist you considerably in being able to recognize bits and pieces of *Real Reality* when it wafts across one's vision (physical or otherwise).

The important thing to realize here is that there is nothing to actually fear in either the *Real Reality* or the *physical universe trance states*. We can face **anything**. There is **no way** we can be hurt. A *being* cannot be destroyed, hurt or trapped. He can experience the **experience** of being destroyed, hurt or trapped if he so wishes or if someone has overwhelmed him and told him he can be so overwhelmed.

We can perceive parts of *Real Reality* that we feel we are not "ready" for. We are, in fact, ready for anything we can see or otherwise perceive. We may think we do not **want** to see what we are seeing, but we **are** ready for it.

Filtering

There are times when our first glimpse of the *Real Reality* concept or idea is so different that we do not have an accurate view of it. We may go for weeks or months with a distorted translation of what we have seen . . . then out of the blue comes the actual concept and we are happy with it. Do not worry if this happens. Changing one's mind about things is all a part of growth on this plane. The exercise itself is good for us.

Misunderstanding or "coloring" communications from other realms is called "filtering." We tend to filter communications that come through to fit our already-decided-upon personal philosophies. When we get a communication that doesn't fit the mold, we tend to bend it slightly in an effort to **make** it fit. This is usually an unconscious activity since we really do want to know the truth. The more one becomes enlightened, the less one filters.

Hallucinatory Reality

It is possible to go into deeper and deeper *physical universe trance states* and "feel" as though one is connecting with *Real Reality*. This occurs in cases of insanity and in periods of giddy unreality brought on by hysteria, great stress, injury, chemical damage, drugs or alcohol. In such states the individual may become heavily emotional, sad and fearful, in a coma or a catatonic state. The person may reach a point of terror or of not caring about anyone or anything and feeling "swept away" — released of all responsibility.

Strangely enough, there are those who **have** connected with *Real Reality* under just the same circumstances as described above. There are those who read this book knowing that what they have experienced is *Real Reality*.

"Bad trips" or frightening hallucinations on drugs or alcohol, or even the results of suggestion during hypnosis or frenzy are definitely due to dipping down into deeper physical universe altered states. At such times one may have the feeling of being shot out or forced out of the body.

When We Choose to Enter This Universe

The *physical universe trance state* is entered into with complete willingness by each of us. We know full well what the ground rules are and also the types of experiences we are likely to encounter. We choose the dimension, universe or world in which we wish to play a game in physical form. We choose the form — be it tiger, plant or human — male or female. We decide upon the period (dates) we wish to visit; upon the planet, race, continent, section of the country, city, town or rural area; upon parents and many times brothers or sisters, or even neighbors who perhaps are old friends.

We may choose a family that is very poor in worldly goods but rich in spirit, or a family that is rich in worldly goods and very poor in spirit, or any possible combinations of that idea. We may choose a family that will make life very difficult, giving us great barriers to overcome at an early age, thus making success all the sweeter. There are millions of considerations that are involved in the choosing of an Earth-family and situation.

We may choose to play games totally opposite to the one we played before. In one life perhaps we were slave owners. The next life on this plane could very well be spent as a slave. We change back and forth between male and female existences — we change races, countries, caste systems and even body impairments.

Now, it is true that while we choose our birth situations, etc., we do not write the complete scenario. If we have decided to begin with great difficulties, then we might well expect hardships as babies and children. We do not say, for instance, that we are going to be abused physically and emotionally by beatings at an early age. What we would most likely have decided was that we wanted to experience great depth of feeling early in life in order to accomplish understanding and enlightenment before ending that lifetime. Perhaps we have become partially enlightened while in a body and wish to complete enlightenment this time at an early age. Whatever the reason, we always choose.

There are so many goals possible on this plane that we become curious about them and wish to experience them. Once we look at the fact that hardships are not necessarily negative experiences, but opportunities for growth **through** experience, we can begin to gain the unique position of viewing a part of *Real Reality*.

On the other side of the coin, we see that our parents also choose us, no matter how it may seem. We serve one another in many ways. Some mothers are chosen in order to merely give us a strong body. We come to our chosen parents sometimes by circuitous routes. A young mother may give her baby over for adoption and the parents who wanted it will come along. Get the idea? There are no accidents when it comes to our most meaningful relationships. We do not come here and leave it all up to chance. We seldom take it that lightly.

This is not to say that **nothing** is left open to chance, because it is — but nothing as important as our beginnings which carry with them the best launching pad for the viewpoints from which we wish to live a life.

All through life we will find chance events and people wafting in and out, but rarely do they figure strongly in our life choices. One can see that these choices do not lock us into ironclad events and results. The closer we are to awakening, the more power we have over these events. As we become more powerful over our own lives and events, the less we really have to experience pain in order to grow. The closer we are to awakening, the more easily we can begin to grow through joy.

Is it not wonderful to think that we can choose our parents even if they are unable to bear children? We simply have to find someone who is willing to give us a body and make it possible for our chosen parents to find us. This is all done telepathically and is rarely perceived by the *beings* involved, at least on an analytical level.

We are not separate and we are constantly agreeing to help one another in one way or another. We are constantly appearing at just the right moment to make a difference in someone's life. Never mind whether or not it "seems" to be negative. The need is still there.

The Age We Choose

It is no accident that you are living where you are now at this time and if you are reading this book from a viewpoint of reality, you most probably even know your mission or goals for this life or are close to finding out. Perhaps you have always known.

This is a most exciting age in which to live. We have many surprises and adventures awaiting us in the near future. The climate for spiritual growth and enlightenment is burgeoning with new heights and depths of freedoms to think and grow that are unparalleled in any cycle on this planet.

The emergence of the United States of America as a free nation was a deliberate move on the overall game board or jigsaw puzzle of life on this planet. All *beings* here were involved with its creation. The very idea that large groups of people could live together and not only think freely but act upon their thoughts! If you think you are not free, all you have to do is recall the past. It is sometimes hard to remember just how bad it was even at the turn of this century.

All the pictures have faded to comforting sepia tones, leaving us with romantic ideas of the times in which "life was simpler," easier somehow.

What is left now are a few tremors within the ranks of civilization as we know it — a few more challenging experiences yet to come, but an overall look tells volumes about us as a people. And our future is bright. We need to exercise our freedoms and make them grow stronger.

There have been and are still other movements in other countries with similar objectives. All the pieces will begin to come together, and within ten years the master plan will be visible to those who can look and see. New hopes and certainty will spring up, all apology for spiritual realities and enlightening knowledge will fade away, and all we have worked for will come to life.

Order

It is difficult to see any kind of order when there is so much misery in this world, but we are all busy in our dream states, working as one with our multidimensional realities to keep our game going in some kind of cohesive manner. We are all a part of what is happening here.

The order that we see in this universe is the product of intricate agreements affected by telepathy between all *beings* operating on this plane. This thread of telepathic communication lies below our conscious levels of understanding and necessarily so since it leaves our conscious awareness free to create games and relationships without being hampered with the inner workings of the material universe. This is similar to the way the autonomic aspect of our bodies, such as heartbeat, blood flow, breathing and glandular secretions are taken care of for us so we can "play" without watching the store, so to speak.

Belonging

At one time or another we each feel as though we shouldn't be here on this planet, in this city or country, and even especially in this particular family. That is because, as hard as we try not to, we have glimpses into other realms but are unable to decipher their meaning. The truth is that we are all welcomed and a place is **always** made for us. If it were not, no one could see or hear us. No one would bear us as children. In other words, we would merely be wispy projections.

The intricacies of creating life as we know it are myriad and so complex that they literally cannot be fully perceived by those participating in it. We simply cannot become objective enough to see it all. We have to remove ourselves entirely from this dimension in order to view it as it is. However, if we could view it from here, in that manner, we could no longer be involved intimately with this *third dimension*. We would more than likely leave the body at once because we would have come out of the *physical universe trance state* in order to see these complexities.

So, if you are here and if you are involved in life at all, then you **do belong**. Many times our goals are long in coming and it seems we will never experience those things we wish to experience, but it does not mean we do not belong — for indeed we do.

Our being here has importance to the whole network of life here. Each **place** is assured and is a part of the whole *third dimensional* experience.

Experience and Growth

No one is native to this universe or any other physical universe for that matter. We *beings* are greedy for experience and learning about different viewpoints. We try many games in order to satisfy this appetite. We use raw materials provided by the *Creator* and we create this world over and over again each moment or it would not persist very long. We sort of make things up as we go along, laying our "tracks" before us in order to have something to step upon. Knowing this, we can learn to lay our tracks before us and place on those tracks all the things and happenings hoped for in life. There is more on this subject later in the book.

We choose one probable action or result over another, thus forming a cohesive whole. The formulae are well known by all of us, but for purpose of a rather "hide and seek" kind of existence which those in physical form seem to prefer, such answers are not readily available or even necessary for the time being.

One might think that it is the physical experience itself which brings about our growth, but it is the entirety of what is happening in this as well as on the spiritual plane, throughout all dimensions, that signals success or failure of a particular game plan. There is no actual failure, however, only degrees of success. There are degrees of grace — that is to say, the **way** in which we fulfill our goals that signals the depth of our growth in enlightenment.

Oneness

The idea of oneness is difficult to describe in this physical universe but not impossible. One does not **create** oneness. One **experiences** it. **Knows** it. It already exists.

With the emergence of the realizations of oneness, the depth of our growth in enlightenment becomes ever richer and deeper. With the actual *knowingness* of the existence of the kinship of *All There Is*, the scope of our understanding grows and grows and cannot ever be stopped once it begins. We become relentless in our reach for more.

Imagine a large harp with many strings. Now, imagine taking your thumb and strumming from top to bottom. Each string has its own vibration. Each string has its own existence separate, yet as a part of the whole, each string sets up vibratory harmonics in the other. The experience of such a strumming with the waves of sound and sensation, harmonics, even color, is very similar to the effect our thoughts and actions have. When we think of another, we are literally vibrating some part of their universe. When we have thoughts that are disturbing, then that vibration actually does affect the other *being* on some level. Conversely, when we send healing and thoughts of love, these too are felt.

If you really think you are separate, try this. Recall a time when you did a cruel thing to someone weaker than you or someone you loved and then tried to convince yourself you were unaffected. You really tried to convince yourself you were **totally** unaffected.

The vibrations experienced between you were real. No amount of hiding will completely erase the effects of your thoughts, either within yourself or the other person. If you were not connected, then how could such a phenomenon occur? What do you think the vibrations traveled upon? They traveled upon those invisible chords that connect us, one to the other. Remember the harp? Each string is separate, yet connected by the body of the harp to every other string.

Even plants are sensitive to emotions of those who care for them. It has been discovered in laboratory experiments that plants belonging to an individual will react with measurable electrical impulses when the owner is upset, hurt or otherwise emotional, even if separated by great distance. Plants are also sensitive to trauma of other life forms in their vicinity.

Privacy and Thoughts

The whole idea of "privacy" is part and parcel of the considerations that we are separate and that our thoughts cannot or should not be known to others. On this physical plane it makes us nervous to think that even our thoughts can be monitored somehow, that is until we understand that "thoughts" create physical particles. Intense thoughts create objects and events with the use of these particles. This is the raw stuff of which our physical reality is made. It is true, that the "intent" rather than the "content" of our thoughts is what is perceived by those who "hear" what we are thinking.

Our thoughts are "felt" by those of whom we are thinking. For instance, if we think of Betty in an angry way, Betty "feels" it on one level or another. Probably not on any conscious level, but she is aware of it nonetheless. If we think of Betty in glowing terms, she also perceives that, and her life is enhanced by the energy in the thought. Conversely, the energy sent forth in the angry thought will impinge in a "negative" way.

Now, if we are horrified by these thoughts and look back, realizing that our thoughts have had some impact upon a *being* that we did not really intend, we can "erase" the effects by sending out "positive" thoughts toward Betty.

Once a thought has occurred, it sets forth on a life of its own. Our thoughts create particles that are picked up on this and other planes and used to create object and events. There is no judgment involved in the content of the original thought. It simply becomes raw material for other creations on this as well as other planes. Likewise, particles of thought enter our dimension as raw material for creation. For instance, color and light are products of thought processes from other dimensions.

Oneness and Differing Realities

Oneness already exists. We do not invent it when we become aware. We reexperience that part of *Real Reality*.

> The awareness of the connection to *All There Is* begins with the awareness of the connection to any part of it.

To many, the experiences of separateness and loss comprise the totality of life and **everything** is filtered through this spectrum. When we talk with them, we can see and feel the pain of their realities. All efforts to get them to think positively are met with heavy resistance and even suspicion. The more time we spend with them, the more feeling of loss we begin to experience for ourselves. They are residing in a part of the *physical universe trance state* from which they simply cannot share your realities.

The idea that relationships are so terribly difficult to establish and maintain because we are all so different does have some validity. If, however. we can look at oneness in a slightly different way, perhaps we can begin to see hope for it yet.

How, one thinks, can there possibly be a feeling of oneness with one who is so totally different? For example — a race car driver may find it difficult to share ideas, concepts or even dinner with a derelict woman from the streets of Chicago. She would find it equally difficult to share ideas and concepts with him, and dinner would be out of the question. Yet, both *beings* may even come from the same *spirit family*. How, then, can we even **begin** to relate with one another with feelings and experiences of oneness?

Let's take away from these two hypothetical opposites all that belongs to the physical universe — clothes, views, ideas, family background, life experiences, goals, games, misunderstandings, understandings, unawarenesses, opinions, realities, belongings, bodies, problems — and what do we have left? Ah ha! The *being* who is relating to all universes, being responsible for all happenings everywhere, totally perfect, beautiful, knowing, understanding, growing ever and always as all *beings* grow, and is connected to *All There Is* knowingly and is in tune with the inner *beingness* of self and others — that is what is left.

Oneness and the Reality of Life on This Plane

When we speak of *Oneness*, we are speaking of *Oneness* **outside** of the physical universe. Aspects of physical life such as goals and personality do not have to be agreed upon in order for us to be able to connect with the *inner beingness* of another. Otherwise we would constantly trip over one another's game here. We **do** come here to **experience** privacy, secrecy, mystery, but this does not necessarily mean we have to be separate.

We can experience *Oneness* without having to agree with the **details** of how the other is choosing to experience life on this plane. The race car driver can look at the derelict woman and love her for what she really is and admire her for the game she is playing. She is playing it so convincingly that there is very little in common between her game and his. He is playing his role so convincingly that she cannot find any common ground between them at all. And yet, there is great recognition between them. They are aware of one another and aware of physical universe differences. They may even be convinced that these differences are **real**.

A further look at this concept shows us how we can feel a *Oneness* with all life without having to participate with the various aspects of other life forms. We can enjoy animals without having to agree with their practices concerning the expelling of body wastes. We can co-exist with them and teach them ways of being appreciative of our ways of life in exchange for being cared for. We do not have to live in a bird cage in order to feel at one with a bird. We do not have to live in a fish tank trying to learn how to breathe under water in order to experience oneness with fish.

It is a point of view. We are one in spirit. It does not involve intimate sharing of each other's games or goals. When we find someone with similar goals, it is exciting and the feeling of oneness seems easier, but we can experience *Oneness* with all of life everywhere — even dimensions with which we have no memory. We can **know** more than we can **see**. So it is our *knowingness* we need to exercise and to which we must give acknowledgment.

> *Oneness* is **experienced** from within. *Oneness* **lives** within. In order to experience and understand oneness one can look within and find the core of one's own being and find that core to be the common reality which we all share.

There are many ways in which we vibrate and experience that common core but there is none more delightful and enlightening as shared laughter at the same joke. Recall the swelling in the chest, the sudden rise in temperature and the deepness of breath. Recall the feeling of kinship with all others around you who are laughing. The feeling is that of oneness and almost unparalleled delight and release.

We experience it in other ways — always with shared **feelings**. This is the key to tapping into *Oneness* on this plane. **Feelings**.

Perhaps a first step toward understanding oneness could be to practice perceiving the *inner being* of all people and all life. When we do, we are closer to communicating with it and therefore closer to communicating with our own *inner beingness* — and that, my friends, is the open sesame to happiness, growth, abundance and success even in physical universe terms.

Tapping into Real Reality

A good way to communicate the concept of tapping into *Real Reality* is to enlist your participation. There are many times in our lives that we experience our "higher selves" or "higher awarenesses" during involvement with aspects of this universe when we were deeply moved by someone or some occurrence. You may or may not have felt yourself lifting above or out of your body or diving joyfully deep into your own private universe where everything is perfect, but you can most certainly recall feeling a moment of intense elation that swept you for a time definitely into a different "place."

Perhaps you were even moved to tears. It could have been during the playing of your national anthem or a poignant scene in a movie or play, upon receiving a surprise gift from someone important to you, or upon holding your own child for the first time.

During such a moment, you were experiencing *Real Reality*. All the mundane, heavy everydayness is not reality but by-products of the physical universe and has genesis in this world's pretend-reality. The experience of *Real Reality* is so fulfilling and relieving that anything we **can** do to experience even a little of it, we **will** do. The search for self, the drive to achieve, thrilling adventure, the acquiring of material things, falling in love, creating effects upon others, helping others, sharing thoughts and realities with others, searching for a soul mate or attempting to reacquaint one's self with one's own power and energies — all of these are attempts at experiencing *Real Reality*.

We go about searching for *Real Reality* in many different ways, yet the desire and thrust is the same: **the reconnecting with** *Real Reality*.

The desire to reexperience *Real Reality* over and over by experiencing times in which we feel moved is most nearly expressed through aesthetics — art, music, theater, landscaping, great architecture and even the way we decorate our living spaces. Some observe nature or meditate. All these endeavors encourage us to have those moments of being lifted out into the more beautiful reality that we have temporarily suspended in order to experience a physical existence.

People have sought these moments and prized them so much that they have taken potions and drugs in the hope that by inducing them artificially, they will last in reality. Some claim success, but the quality of life on this plane begins to deteriorate with the taking of stimulants which are damaging to the psyche's connection with the body. One then has to take more and more and stronger and stronger doses or stronger drugs in an effort to satisfy the desire for release from the confines of this plane.

When we reach *Real Reality*, naturally, without drugs, we see this world not as a place to get away from, but a challenge and adventure full of beauties and other *beings*. Our view becomes healthier, more loving, more understanding and more connected to *All There Is*.

Each of us seeks our own favorite outlet that most nearly transports us into the reality from which we sprang. Some gain it more easily in music or theater, contemplating and enjoying nature, meditating, while others may get it from being thrilled by sports, or by great physical exertion, being frightened by monster movies, ghost stories or even through sexual expression.

Some have created barriers — so many barriers from themselves that the only way they can be transported is to take active, violent measures against others or the property of others in order to be moved at all — in order to feel alive at all. Such people believe that they **are** matter, energy, space and time. They have forgotten that they are *spirits* and that they are a part of *All There Is*.

They may even think they are the only ones alive and that the rest of the people and objects are just solid parts of an alien world that is all too threatening and strange. In other words, such *beings* are not relating to others at all but are experiencing intense, painful separateness and isolation. They are living in deep *physical universe* *trance states*.

There are those few, however, who live on the "edge" and they derive deep emotional satisfactions from courting danger. These are our race car drivers, mountain climbers, explorers and may even include some hobos, gamblers and others who live totally unpredictable lives.

Success

One who is seeking to relate only to other worlds and dimensions in the hope of escaping the problems in this one is in for a rude shock. We **are** here to play games, not squirm out when the going gets rough. It is really all right to play earthly games and enjoy them. There is great joy to be derived in having concourse with the peoples of this universe and this planet in particular.

It is **not** a degrading thing to enjoy having a body, to enjoy sex, being ill, being poor, having no earthly goods, being uneducated...Nothing on earth is degrading. We simply are playing those games in order to find out about them — to learn from them. At the same time, we cannot expect everyone to be interested in the same game.

It is not even degrading to have a physical impairment or to be mentally retarded. In fact, there may be great courage and heroism involved both by the sufferer and by those who aid such a *being*, whether it be plant, animal or human. It is not degrading to have a body and to play games on this plane. Besides, we are a part of it all and we are a part of the creation of *All There Is*, so why deny ourselves the fruits of our own creations?

If we are playing any games at all on this plane, we are succeeding. If we are rich, we are succeeding at being rich. If we are poor, we are succeeding at the game of being poor. If we are terrifically endowed with physical beauty, we are succeeding at being physically beautiful. If we are terrifically physically impaired, we are succeeding at the game of survival with physical impairment. The end result that is being sought may not always be laughter and happiness. The end result could very well be the appreciation of the heavier emotional experiences.

Now, we can sit around making so many judgments about one another and the games everyone is playing that we miss opportunities for our growth experiences. We can get so caught up in the struggle to achieve what we think we want that we miss all the beauty and happiness that lies just outside our peripheral vision. We sometimes get so busy plowing straight ahead that we miss all the fun that lies just on the other side of our blinders.

We Always Win

We may live a life of great sorrow, trouble, injury, loss of love and limb — and yet, **no matter how it looks** to others at our time of death, we all win. The idea that we all lose because we all end up losing our bodies and don't fulfill this-universe goals is a false one. Our real goals are not dependent upon any society's standards. They are not even dependent upon keeping a body. Society's standards are born exclusively out of an economic idea of success and security as is related to earning power, celebrity power and the possession of worldly goods. That does not mean to say that everyone with a great deal of money is not winning at a game. All that is meant is that the possession of money, power or fame does not automatically signal a winning game. One's game could be totally separate to the amount of money amassed.

Success and Physical Health

Physical health does not signal the presence of spiritual growth or awareness any more than ill health is the sign of a sick mind. Illness can sometimes force introspection and contemplation of life goals and purposes. Illness can often serve as a catalyst to further understandings and realizations. The experience itself can help produce compassion, patience toward others and even toward oneself. Illness is used also by a *being* simply as a barrier to be overcome. An adventure.

The game of attaining body health is just as worthy a game as any other. The discipline necessary to fulfill one's goals in this area is very great and the success is sweet also. There are those who consider body health to be a way of opening up to awareness. It certainly can be, but there are many other ways as well. Even the discipline of body desires and the self-denial can be cleansing if not pushed too far. But to think one's body is the way to awareness is as unreal as thinking one can find happiness in **any** physical object.

Life as a Recluse

Success is not precluded for one who becomes a monk or recluse, avoiding as much physical universe stimuli as possible. It is as if one goes to a party and hides in the closet. Although, such a life can well be enjoyed as a resting period after or before lives of tremendous hardship or unpredictability. There are those who live such restricted lives in order to learn by them, so our example is not one of judgment against such persons.

There are so many games, so many opportunities to learn and experience on this plane, that humankind is determined to exhaust each possibility. And that is the way we set it up, so why not?

Reaching final awareness is not a race or competition. We are not **above** those who are not ready for awakening. The ultimate and sweetest success is finding our way back to the connection with **All There Is.**

Puberty

Another way in which we relate to this world is to set about trying to bring about changes. We decide what is best for us and therefore for all of humankind. We have great resources for effecting these changes. One of the greatest is puberty — or rather the power unleashed by us at this time of life.

By beginning to introduce spiritual realities and values into the lives of our children, we are going to have an easier time of it in regard to bringing about changes.

The young are still operating on the energies that are released at birth. These energies, for the most part, lie dormant until puberty. If not given a positive *channel* of outlet, these energies will be wasted and used for mischief or can be discharged in criminal and destructive ways.

Some adolescents become so frustrated with this energy that they develop the uncanny poltergeist type of ability to hurl objects around the room, sending dishes crashing to the floor or producing knocking sounds behind walls and under floors.

Others tend to discharge their energies in sports and mischief. Our children are not aware of the nature of these energies, and the adolescents are totally unaware that **they** are the ones responsible for the flying objects.

It is important to note that these energies are not evil in nature but are a part of a deep reservoir of raw energy. Some *beings* recognize the power in themselves and respond to it responsibly. These are the unusual children who seem to be more mature. They set about creating projects and applying themselves to humanitarian or other productive endeavors. They are most often *beings* who are perhaps higher on the rung of development than the others. They are not better people, just further along.

This raw energy was initially intended and used to launch the child into responsible adulthood. It provided them with the active thrust necessary to break away from childish pursuits and with the confidence to begin forming adult decisions, learning to trust in the self.

Knowing this, it is clear why there is so much frustration in our young people today. They come through puberty unleashing all this power and are told they are still children, unable to make decisions, unready to find their own place in the world, mistrusted for the energy itself.

There are some remote tribes even today that recognize this powerful energy and have actual ceremonies in which these energies are focused productively, not only for the individual but for the whole tribe, giving it new life and expansion. The entire tribe receives endowments of energies during such ceremonies and joyful celebration lasts for days.

This is not to say that our children must be made to take full responsibility for the changes we wish to bring about in our world, even though in a sense that is why they are here. But children also fare much better when they are allowed to use their power of joy and spirit of play. These qualities are greatly accelerated at puberty (some even earlier) and last sometimes into the twenties.

The creative aspects of this period in their lives can bring about long-lasting sense of self-worth, confidence and a great sense of fulfillment if not tampered with in ways that take away self-reliance and self-determination. It would be sad, indeed, if in an effort to help them tap into these energies we sent them into ultraserious endeavors.

The freedom to experiment and learn of altered states, **naturally induced**, could be a great step toward the end of the use of drugs by our most precious resource — our children.

There seems to be fear that these energies could lead to "evil" use of powers when, in fact, "evil" is the product of the **unaware**. But, of course, evil is a relative term and isn't "real" except in "lower" levels of consciousness.

Religion and Freedom

It is true that many of us have used religion as a stepping-stone to further spiritual awareness. Most religions or practices can be of great help, but due to further spiritual growth the *being* is eventually ready to go on to another path. This is most usually the case. It does not mean that one cannot acknowledge the gain received from one practice which has led to further growth in another direction.

Spirit guides remain above and beyond religious beliefs and there is great allowance given to each *being* to follow a religion or not. You will find that your *guides* may never try to influence you in this matter at all. On the other hand, if asked, they will give objective advice which can be of help in deciding for oneself just what to do about a particular religious practice. Any practice which is serving as a reinforcement for the *being* and is a sustaining factor or serves as a fertile field for challenge and growth will get "good marks" from your *guides*.

Many of our most important lessons are learned under the banner of religion. The barriers and challenges that are inherent in a religious practice which seeks to control the actions and thoughts of its members can actually serve as perfect vehicles with which to realize our basic freedoms. Sooner or later each *being* will look up and realize he is already free — and free without the help of an organization or group, but by and for the "self" as a part of *All There Is*.

No person can free another. We might help by recognizing the beauty and existence of one another. We may be able to help another recognize his/her own freedom, but freedom and entrapment are both attained through the use of the mind, and human beings love to use their minds. They use them to create ideas and futures. They also use them to create barriers. And whatever is created can be uncreated.

It would appear that *beings* love to fight over and over for their freedoms to think, travel, speak and act as they choose. In reality, there is no way one can **not** be free to think, travel, speak and act as one chooses. If we are willing to sacrifice all that our societies hold dear, including our bodies, there is no end to our freedoms.

It is tempting to think that there is only **one way** to free ourselves from the dreadful future that is most certainly ours if we fail to adhere to one single philosophy. Yet, we see those all around us who do not believe as we do who are surviving very well, indeed, with a lot going for them in terms of security, a certain amount of happiness and success in their terms. Who can know what is in another's heart or to what degree another *being* has progressed in awareness?

It is not necessary for *beings* to be afraid or suspicious of those whose beliefs differ. We are **all** constantly experimenting. Experimenting with one idea or avenue after another. The details are often going to go counter to others around us.

The freedom of our young to experiment and fulfill their own destinies is important for all of us. They are *travelers* who have their own reasons for coming here and who have their own games to play. The best we can do is tell them the truth as we know it and allow them to experiment with knowledge of probable effects. We can help them understand the nature of the vast power of their unleashed energies and help them channel those energies in creative and productive ways.

Laying Our Tracks

Our environment becomes just what we believe it will become. We shape it every day in a million ways. We send out commands in the form of belief-based expectations and when they come true, we are generally surprised.

The intensity of our desires and the intensity of our intentions will greatly influence the speed at which we grow. The willingness to peer into other dimensions and other realities will serve to propel us forward in our own games.

We do orchestrate our own lives whether we are aware of it or not. If we do not grow and become more aware of this point, we will have times in which we lose control over happenings and events that shape our "futures." We fall through the cracks, so to speak, and depend upon the ebb and flow of the lives of others to shape our own.

Falling through the Cracks

We have all had such experiences of losing control of our lives. These periods come as a direct result of lack of planning and conscious placing there by intention what we want to have happen. In a sense, we lay our tracks before us just before we step. Now, if we fall off the tracks altogether, we "fall through the cracks" and the cracks can be very deep. There are times when we need such an experience to force us to look up from the depths for some greater concept to hang on to — some higher ideal to urge us on. We may merely want to know how it feels to have such an experience. It is a sort of grab-bag period of existence.

Walking Others' Tracks

We can also experience walking on someone else's tracks but we must give over our self-determination in order to make it work. If there is enough similarity between the game plans of two individuals, they may construct the tracks together for a period of time and never feel deprived of self-determination. But the time generally comes when one wishes to split off and begin to lay other, more individual tracks in order to grow. It may happen in this lifetime or in the next or next.

Men often expect to lay tracks for themselves and their wives. But when the wife has a strong *game plan* of her own, it sooner or later becomes necessary for her to create a life of her own. At such times, both partners will sometimes think that she has changed, but it is only a natural next step in her development and most probably also for his. This doesn't always mean that the marriage is over. It could, but it could also mean greater scope and renewed interest in one another and in the game they have set up together.

Parents often want to lay tracks for their children and are so surprised when they find their offspring are unwilling to walk those tracks. To an extent, it is necessary for parents to guide their children along "made-up" tracks until they are able to lay their own with some degree of wisdom. It is also important for parents not to expect their children to decide upon their futures at early ages.

The Vastness of Self

If we expect to have freedoms, then we must extend freedoms to others. Prior to realizing our own powers and before understanding the nature of what constitutes the totality of our own being we rarely "tune in" to our own natural freedoms. As a result, we manifest unwillingness to grant full freedom to others. We justify this usually by mistrusting others to use freedoms wisely.

These attitudes are the result of the lack of an ability to recognize the scope and vastness of the self and that of others. The idea that the **whole** being is the personality that directs and uses a body is the basic idea that gets us into trouble. For us to deny our vastness is similar to having a hair on the head deny the existence of the rest of the body.

We are so vast as *beings* that our strength and power if totally unleashed upon this plane would cause energy vortexes of devastating power unparalleled in any universe.

Imagine, if you will, a man 75,000 feet tall trying to step into a doll's house without wrecking it. That is a pale description of the wide disparity between the power and size of a being and the size of this universe. This universe is so small that in order for us to play in it we must miniaturize a tiny part of ourselves. We simply dip a toe into it. When we dip our big toe into the water the whole body experiences it — the warmth, the wetness, the delightful sensation — it is the same with the way we dip a small part of ourselves into the physical universe, planet Earth.

Now, our big toe is in no way totally representative of our body as a whole, yet it is a very real and vital part of the structure. Our big toe cannot understand the vastness of the whole body any more than we can totally understand the vastness of our whole being as long as we are in a *physical universe trance state*.

> No one can tell us in truth that we can never know ourselves. It simply isn't true. **We can not but know ourselves**.

We are so vast as *beings* that our strength and power, vitality and love can change entire worlds. We can change our worlds into whatever we wish them to be. We can change this one into a world of peace, love, unity, laughter and fun. We can learn to create art so devastatingly wonderful that people will stand for days looking at it without moving. We can create a world that **almost** reflects our vastness as *beings*. There is no physical plane that can fully reflect us as we really are. All that we are simply cannot be reflected or contained in any physical universe.

Now, when we refer to this world as small and ourselves as large, understand that these are terms relative to the physical universe only. Large and small are comparative terms and are only of value in the describing of physical structures. There is no measure of the "size" of a *being*. But for purposes of laying out a concept, these are the criteria upon which we can share reality with you.

The use of a jet engine to power a child's tricycle would certainly result in its destruction as well as part of the neighborhood. The size, thrust and power of a *being* if introduced fully into this plane would simply annihilate it.

We Relate to This Universe In Several Ways

1. Temporary and partial suspension of *Real Reality*.
2. Telepathic recognition of its structure and content.
3. Energy thrusts from *inner beingness* to physical body.
4. Telepathic recognition of societal agreements.
5. Willingness to play the game of physical existence and take the inherent consequences of it.
6. Telepathic agreements concerning the laws of this universe — just how far we will or will not stretch the laws in order to satisfy our goals.

Harmony

The challenge now is to find ways of living, loving and growing in harmony — enjoying each other and each other's differences. One is fearful of the differences in others because of the insecurities within the self. To one who is secure within and ready for change — welcoming it — then the differences of others are exciting, even thrilling. Never threatening. Other's ideas are threatening only when one's own ideas are shaky or doubtful.

To learn to live in harmony while maintaining individual choice of accepting or not accepting the ideas of others and to be willing to grant freedoms to others is to live in **heaven on earth**. And this is what each of us is working toward, no matter how it looks to others.

> The true appreciation of the spirit within each personality over and above any social idea or action takes us all into a new dimension of understanding.

We have not even begun to tap the potentialities that lie within easy grasp of one who is truly connected by *knowingness* to *All There Is*. To a whole society or planet connected to *All There Is*, we can find power and beauty that will catapult this entire universe into a completely new state of being with new potentials, new goals, new growth undreamed of since the beginning of creation in this dimension. The great experiment with the *third dimension* will indeed come into its own, bearing fruits of stunning beauty and excitement.

CHAPTER FOUR

THE ANATOMY OF THE SPIRIT WORLD

All *beings* are **individuals**. We always were and always will be. We will never merely "melt" into some enormous glob of *beings* and forget that we ever existed. That which is **you**, now, will always be.

Due to the nature of *beingness*, on this plane, we think we have to be totally separate in order to be individuals, yet we **are** *all there is*. If you continue to think upon this concept, it will eventually come into focus. There is no earthly language to describe *Real Reality*. We can come close and in further contemplation we begin to focus and understand.

Throughout existence, we may from time to time elect to become a part of a larger movement and sway with a group, but these groups depend upon each individual's power and thrust for life — no matter the plane within which it resides for the moment. And for that power to be viable, it must be given freely. It cannot be taken.

We will never lose our status as individuals. We may change our personalities, our aims and goals, our directions, but we are always and forever — ourselves.

In reality, there are many more *beings* without bodies than with bodies. Beings from time to time decide to play a game that is connected to a type of physical existence. We wish to enrich our collection of experiences for purposes of growth and for the experience itself.

From time to time we decide to connect only slightly to a solid existence and may choose to guide one who takes up a body. In that way, our experiences can be shared and our lives sculpted to suit the purposes of more than one *being* at a time. This does not in any way take away from our own determinism.

There seems to be a cardinal rule that the *spirit guides* can only be perceived when the *being* who has the body or other solid connection is ready to acknowledge their existence.

Another rule seems to be that the "game" decided upon by the *traveler* is the game that is played. In other words, the *spirit guides* do not try to change the game but are wholly intent upon aiding in the game as originally agreed upon.

Viewpoints

Actually, the *spirit world*, isn't a **place**, but a multiplicity of **viewpoints**. There are many millions of *beings* who never pay even the slightest attention to our dimension at all. Indeed, there are as many universes as there are points of view. And by universes we don't mean star systems. There are many physical universes similar to this one and many not so similar. There are physical universes heavier and many lighter. Some of these dimensions are so wispy that we could hardly see them at all. Ours is not the heaviest by far. Some are so heavy that our present bodies would appear as ghosts had we the ability to travel there.

There are dimensions upon dimensions. There are as many viewpoints as can be imagined and almost as many worlds. And yet, we are all as much a part of one as the other. These dimensions interact with one another in a myriad of ways. There is no way that any part of *All There Is* can be cut off and exist separately.

Real reality is not a place. It encompasses physical universes and nonphysical universes as well and all imagination, creation and thought. You might say that *All There Is* describes **everything**. *Real reality* describes viewpoints of *All There Is*. What **is**, is. But how we view it makes up *Real Reality*. Growth occurs within *Real Reality*. Even our *physical universe trance states* are created from *Real Reality*.

You might say that *physical universe trance states* are unreal reality, created solely for the purpose of challenge and surprise. For us to be surprised we must suspend the state of *Real Reality* to some degree, depending upon the game and the desired result as well as the dimension.

What we do here affects all other dimensions. All existence is a vast recycling plant, in a manner of speaking. Nothing is wasted and all particles merely change and become raw materials for the creation of other particles or vibrations or influences, from one dimension to the other. Just as we wave our arm and hand in the air and are unable to see the hundreds of waves and eddies that form as a result, we are unable to see the destiny of our thoughts, flows and even our realizations and daydreams.

Due to the nature of the differences in dimensions — and add to that the *physical universe trance state* which we have assumed — it is difficult to view interdimensionally while in the body. It is easiest when the body is asleep and we are free to waft back and forth from one world to another. At times, we even "remember" another world experience or "dream" for a moment, but it quickly fades because of our inability to translate the experience in terms of the laws of **this** universe. If we were less connected to the symbolism here, we could better understand the symbolisms of other planes. With practice we can become more sensitive to them and thus enrich our store of knowledge and understanding of *Real Reality*.

Spirit Families, Friends and Guides

There are many large groups of *beings* who, being of like "mind," have gravitated naturally to one another. Actually, the bond is a result of a combination of long-standing partnerships in the playing of games and common interests in shared worlds. There are some *spirit families* that have been formed in infinity and are very old. Some are relatively new. These *families'* members come and go — one *family* to another, fluctuating, visiting other groups and spending "time" in long pursuits on their own or with other *families* or groups. Nothing is cut and dried in the *spirit world*.

Within these *families* are smaller groups comprised of *beings* who are more or less on equal levels of growth and development. The members of these groups are very close spiritually and have played many games on many levels with one another throughout eternity. It is from these smaller groups that we choose our *guides*.

When we speak of "equal growth" or "equal understanding," we are not inferring that some *beings* are "lower" than others. We mean only that some *beings* are traveling various paths together.

Sharing in Game Plans

Our nucleus groups from which our *guides* are chosen have come together to plan the "trails" or "game plans" of adventures that take us from dimension to dimension. Each group has chosen **a** way in which the members wish to experience existence and growth and for a time they are together. At other times they are on different levels or parts of the plan. It is not so much that they progress beyond a level or group but that they step into **different** trails with different experiences possible. In this way we do not all have to subjectively experience all worlds. We are able to share our experiences with our groups.

For example, in earth experience, if one of us experiences the middle ages, all our *Spirit Family* members share in that experience. There are times two or more from the group actually are there together sharing the experience — as husband and wife, dear friends, parent and child — thus creating more than one viewpoint for the entire group to share. Get the idea?

There are so many universes and planes with which we can have experiences that we have devised a way in which we can **share** many experiences with one another and go on to ever greater growth. Eternity is forever and there is no rush. The main idea here is in the **sharing**. . . a thing *beings* love to do!

Each small group within a *family* is experiencing different trails or master plans, yet they can also share experiences group to group. Entire *families* will then share *family* to *family*. In this way we all benefit from all experience through sharing and through this sharing become ever more a subjective part of *All There Is*. In like ways you are sharing with them and they with you.

Unlimited Experience and Imagination

The game will never end because more universes are constantly being created as old universes fall into disuse or are radically changed. In the future, physical universes as we know them will no longer be necessary for the gaining of experience. There will be other more complete and more exciting ways to experience separation, love, lack of love, compassion, lack of compassion, pain, ecstasy and the finding of the way back to *Real Reality*.

Since there is no limit to imagination, creation and experience for *beings*, we find ourselves drawn together for purposes of creating games to play, challenges to face and beauties to experience.

Can you even imagine the impact of the very first creation of music? Or color? Or emotion? These creations represent some of the finest examples of imagination and creation that we know on this plane, yet in other dimensions there are creations of such impact and beauty that one in a *physical universe trance state* would actually fly out of the body and never return to it, so great would be the effect.

Our Growth as a Group

Since our *guides* are involved in the same or similar travelings and are similar to us in growth and understanding, we are all developing at about the same speed (for lack of a better word). Our *guides* are as "brothers and sisters" so to speak, who belong to a much larger group in which there are *beings* in various levels and types of development. This is one reason we must never feel that we are "bothering" our *guides* by asking them for advice or by merely communicating with them. It was agreed upon before we took our present bodies that our *guides* would be playing the game with us.

Together, we decide upon the game to be played and goals to be attained. The final decision, of course, resides with you, the *traveler*. We file a flight plan, so to speak, and in that way our *guides* can always help us keep on course.

Most smaller groups — *friends* — attract to themselves some *beings* of "higher" order to serve as *teachers*. By higher order we simply mean those who have already faced the challenges we are now facing. They have been here and gone. These *beings* are more highly evolved but are interested in helping others in their growth. These *teachers* can be called upon when there are **crucial moments** that need a more concentrated flow of power in order to see us through. They may or may not be members of our own specific *family*.

It is important to note that these crucial moments may not necessarily be moments of great stress in terms of this dimension but may very well come at times that, to us, seem rather dull and uninteresting with nothing happening. They may come at times in our sleep or when we are very busy and are not really spiritually aware for the moment. Such crucial times come as a result of coordinate points in our games and in the games of others close to us or even pivotal points in our society or planet.

Our *spirit families* may be as large as several hundred to many thousands. Sometimes more than one *family* will band together for periods in order to accomplish multidimensional changes or prepare for great changes that are ready to occur.

Different Guides for Different Times

Our *friends* or *guides* usually number from about twenty-eight to forty and among them we will most probably communicate with three or four on a regular basis. There will be times that one *being* will seem to fall into the background for a while and another *guide* will be at the forefront of your consciousness. We each have abilities and interests that are unique and when our needs change, we may find new *beings* with whom to have communication. You may find that you have "favorites" who seem closer to you than the others. Most probably, you have played games together with very favorable mutual response and because of that, you feel closer.

Indeed, we find *beings* among our *friends* who have been close associates through many lifetimes and existences and through many periods in other universes and dimensions. We love each other completely and have vowed to help one another grow through the crucibles inherent in this and many other worlds.

Our *guides* are chosen to reflect various aspects of our "personality-selves" here, encouraging and inspiring each of those aspects as prechosen before taking a body. For example, there may be a *guide* who encourages intellectual pursuits, one who inspires us to create music, one who inspires us to laugh and take life more lightly, and on and on.

From time to time we also can call upon other, more advanced members of our *family* to aid in a new spurt of growth. They may not be *teachers* as such but old *friends* who are willing to lend a hand. We can, in fact, communicate with any *being* in existence. There are no barriers as such, and because *beings* can hold many viewpoints at once, we don't have to worry that they are busy. Any time lag would be due to other, more complex factors than time and you can wait or try again.

The Inner Beingness Contains the Totality of All Experience and Growth

When you call upon a *spirit*, you are calling upon all the collective personalities and *beingnesses*, perceptions and experiences that make up the totality of that *spirit*. For instance, if you call upon Mahatma Gandhi, you would receive communication that benefits from the total experience, growth and understanding that comprises the essence of that entity. You would be unlikely to receive communication from the limited, although wonderfully evolved, viewpoints of his one lifetime as Gandhi, as great as that was. Similarly, one would find great changes having occurred with Edison and a total lack of judgmentalism from Ben Franklin. On the other hand, just because some have left the body doesn't mean they are instantly endowed with all-seeing, all knowing eyes.

If a *being* has left the body but hasn't yet left the *physical universe trance state*, your communications would be reflective of the one personality only. The *being* will, more than likely, be experiencing a greater feeling of freedom, but until she/he has returned *Home* and gone through the *decompression period* (i.e., a period of reorientation into the realities outside the physical world), the ideas, opinions and communications will reflect the just-past earthly life experiences.

Suppose we wanted to speak to the *inner beingness* of one who is presently occupying an Earth-body. There would be communication possible from the being's "higher self" since it is absolutely impossible for a *being* to stuff all of his beingness into any physical universe, much less physical form. Therefore, it is possible that others have been communicating with your higher self. Even more than possible. Such communications need not affect the life or attitudes held by a *being* living in physical form, unless the *being* was ready to be so affected. Realize now, that communication with a "higher self" will be more spiritual in nature than practical in a physical universe sense.

Our Guides Never Interfere with Our Game Plans

We can seek counsel from any *being* or entity and it will gladly give such counsel that will not interfere with our original game plans.

It is as though we are children who have asked to be tied to a tree and have made our playmates promise not to untie us until the game is over, no matter what we say or how much we plead — or as a game in which we can ask for hints but cannot be told point-blank answers.

For instance: A *being* decides to play a game that involves danger — living on the edge. He fully intends to take the consequences inherent in danger...perhaps mountain-climbing or car-racing. The *guides* will aid in the furthering of this game. They do not interfere and keep the body from falling or being killed during the game period. They aid in making the experience more enjoyable and exciting. At the same time, they are enjoying the game involvement.

Our *guides* and other members of our *families* want only what is best for us within the rules of our game as set up. They will never attempt to change the game in midstream, but they will do all they can to encourage us to play it out to finish, even when it results in pain, stress or other hardship.

Game Results

The results of a game are not assessed by this-world standards but rather in the growth and depth of experience. Games are usually set up with outlines and sweeping goals and only rarely with any kind of detail, so that the game can be more interesting. If we knew each step of the way, it wouldn't be very interesting or fulfilling.

Our measure of growth is usually not perceivable in entirety until we have left our physical form and are back *Home* again, at which time we can view our games and lives from a totally objective viewpoint.

Finding Our Friends Again

Most people experience great relief and joy when reunited with their *spirit families*. Life becomes much more bearable and meaningful with the reintroduction of a group to which they "belong" and have belonged for all time before and to come. Many people regain lost confidence in themselves and their goals by knowing that they are not alone, but have others who want only to stand by them.

There are many kinds of *families* and *beings* will find each other over vast distances and times. We may sometimes look for one another lifetime after lifetime or physical existence after physical existence in order to repeat or complete a game once started and perhaps interrupted. We may even look for each other just because of love, respect and desire to have further concourse. We may even temporarily change *families* in order to experience the refreshing differences.

Different Kinds of Families

Some *families* are predominantly occupied with broad, sweeping interests while others are more attuned to the arts, sciences or other pursuits that are not easily translatable here and yet they are **all** involved in the creation of all of these things. They are all involved in the creation of other universes as well. Even old universes may go through great changes as their use becomes limited.

There are those *beings* who are *mavericks* or *loners* who rarely ever "belong" to any one group. They will, from time to time, have concourse with other *mavericks* and with large groups. They may even choose *spirit guides* from a group in which they have common interests. Even if we belong to a particular group, that does not mean we do not get involved with others as well. We may even spend a period as a *maverick*. Even *mavericks* serve often as *guides* to other *mavericks*.

There are whole *families* which are more "highly" evolved than others. Many *beings* hang around the fringes of such groups and work their way in if they so choose. Working one's way in involves growth, of course.

Although our *guides* are equal in growth to ourselves, they are more objective and can see direction and flow more easily. Similar to air traffic controllers who can see flight patterns and help to keep order in the skies, aiding the pilot to avoid other planes or dangerous weather, our *friends* can see where our "flight patterns" are leading us and advise better routes for purposes of furthering our game plans. In this respect they may seem more wise, when in fact they are merely more objective. Their views are not hampered by *physical universe trance states*.

Bear in mind that these descriptions and qualitative designations about *beings* are loosely drawn. Our *friends* are constantly shifting from one system of reality to another and are not "fixed" in a location. They are available through a desire to communicate and are invoked by you, naturally, in a desire for confirmation or validation of game actions. Most of the invocations on your part are subconscious to a depth just barely beyond your consciousness and as soon as you become aware of their existence, you can also then be aware of such invocations consciously.

You Have Always Communicated with Your Friends

In our sleep and reverie times we are communicating with our *friends* freely.

Our *spirit families* encompass many dimensions and realities. They can always be "found" and we can always go *Home*. We can unerringly get back *Home* without any trouble because our *guides* are always ready to lead us there whether in sleep or after terminating the body's life. They help us bridge any period of confusion following the loss of a body.

The old idea that our loved ones or *guides* and *friends* would be beckoning us to leave this existence is a false one. We are here for a purpose and we will leave naturally when that purpose has been fulfilled or when it is decided that it is time to go on to another body in order to continue the cycle started. At any rate, we rarely need any help from our *guides* in this decision unless we have met with violence and are "stuck," so to speak.

It is important to realize that our *guides* are not there to pave the way completely for us and protect us much as parents do when we are small. They are playing the game **with** us, not **for** us and they are not any more powerful than we are. Were it otherwise, we would not have any independence at all and would become unable to move or grow in this existence. They never do anything that would cause us to reduce our own power or that would serve to take power away from us.

Our *guides* have the ability to understand all Earth viewpoints, no matter how different or strange they may be. Our *guides* are also equipped to help us understand viewpoints from just outside our dimension. These abilities are among their greatest values to us.

From time to time, we have been *guides* to our *guides* when they were the *travelers*. In this way, we each exercise our own self-determination.

We can fully understand that their advices will **always** reflect the direction of the game plan as set up. Directions **within** that framework are open to change. It is at those times that the *guides* are most valuable. These are the times when, together, we can find the best direction for the moment. This does not mean that the basic game has been changed.

Guides on This Plane

The more we support each other's games and dreams, the more we are able to grow ourselves. We expand each time we are able to accept the existence and viability of another's viewpoints. And, indeed, we act as *guides* for our earthly friends from time to time. We help them sort out their alternatives until they are able to see them more objectively. We may even find ourselves "inspired" by our own or others' *guides* to say just the right thing at the right time. We have all experienced that phenomenon.

Many times during great stress, our *guides* lead us to *friends* who can help us on this plane. Great stress creates "static" that often interferes with our imaginations and the soft voices of our *spirit guides*, and we need a more solid type of communication in order to become unstuck from a situation in which we find it hard to extricate ourselves.

Many times a *guide* will speak through a friend or even a stranger. We have all experienced the ease with which we seem to bare our souls to a stranger on a plane or bus. They, you may be sure, are equally as surprised at the ease with which they may come up with very good advice. People will be "inspired" to say very specific things. They may even unwittingly answer questions for which you have been searching for answers. There are times when, if we would listen to a child, we would hear pure wisdom. It is all too easy not to listen to someone who seems "simple" or too young, but often they have very viable things to say to us. Our "pride" stands in our way and we are unable to see past this-world considerations.

Our children are as ancient as we are and if unhampered, will enrich our experience manyfold. They are too soon told they are ignorant and that their judgment is faulty. No wonder they go a little insane at puberty.

You can even request of your *guides* that they help a certain person with the right words to help you in times of trouble or when you feel "cut off" from them. Simply use intention that George, or whoever, will say just the right thing at just the right moment that will help you to a realization for which you have been seeking. George need not ever know about it. If he does, he may resist the answer or be self-conscious. His inner self will know about it, to be sure, and he is happy to oblige. You need not feel that you are "using" George. Were the tables turned, imagine how good you would feel to be of service.

With practice, we can learn better how to lean upon our *guides* at times of stress or trouble. It **is** possible to communicate and receive communication no matter the situation. Even through the static. It isn't necessary, however, to think we must always have help from other quarters. But it does help when the going is rough. And it does take practice.

Being Inspired by Our Guides

Everyone has experienced the heady feeling of speaking from an "inspired" point of view and wondering "where did **that** come from?" Our *spirit friends* are helping us out and at the same time enjoying the opportunity to interact in a direct way. Many people write music, books, invent things and have inspired ideas by these means. Many scientists work on "inspiration" much of the time.

We are not merely *channels*, depending upon others for real inspiration. Many times we have acted upon our own inner inspiration to help another. It is important to realize this. Not all inspiration comes from others by any means and we often depend upon our own *knowingness* with great results.

When we **are** *channeling*, however, we are just as much a part of these communications as the *guides* who are inspiring us. We are not husks that can only think through those who are "above" us. These times of inspiration are wonderful and fulfilling. We feel energized by them. They are to be highly prized as times when we are fulfilling our goals in the game. We can also inspire ourselves and those around us, experiencing how it feels to be a *guide*.

The more we communicate with our *guides*, the more often we experience periods of growth and enlightenment. This growth will always stay with us, no matter **what** happens or if we feel we have lost it. It is still there for us and will reemerge.

We Cannot Lose Our Guides

There may be times that we feel we have lost our *guides* or feel cut off. Do not worry. These are periods that have come as the result of an accumulation of events and viewpoints that need to be "shaken up," much as a compost heap must be stirred and remixed in order for further change to take place. Our *guides* are most probably closer and more attentive at these times, urging us on and encouraging us to weather the storm and emerge victorious. They are there, whether we can sense them or not. It is at these times that we most nearly fulfill the original goals of our games. They are actually opportunities to stretch and grow as never before.

The important thing is that we come to realize the potentialities of these hard-to-bear times and consciously use them to further our evolvement.

It may be difficult to imagine that through a period of great stress or even crashing boredom there are wonderful things happening in our universes. It is not always necessary to be suffering in order to grow. It is just that we **also** grow while suffering. We grow in times of great joy and excitement as well. We can even "feel" ourselves enlarging when we are having a good time. We feel ourselves expanding. At these times we grow in confidence and assurance and self-worth.

Truth

When we speak of "truth," we are speaking of the laws that make up *Real Reality*. There are levels aside from or above *Real Reality*. Those levels are unreachable from our physical universe plane, so all we need to concern ourselves with is reaching *Real Reality*. That is our second step. Our first step is to reach our own *inner being* and that is what our *guides* want to help us do.

Many of our *guides* and *friends* are aware of us only on a spiritual level. They are aware of our growth in enlightenment but have little or no interest or information regarding details of our lives here. Then there are those who have lived many lives on this plane and perhaps even recently. These are the ones who are most adept and interested in answering specific questions about earthly problems and concerns.

We can speak with our *guides* and *friends* without fear, without anxiety and with total certainty that they exist and are there for us to turn to when we are ready to grow. When we need companionship — when we need comfort and understanding and love — they are there. They are there for us, enlightening us and being willing to suffer the stresses involved with communicating to this plane. They are unhampered by judgmentalism, self-servingness, bias or criticism. They are truly objective. Their objectivity stems from the fact that they are viewing from *Real Reality* and are not hampered by *physical universe trance states*, considerations and pressures.

Yourself as Guide and Facets of the Self

In the final analysis, the best *spirit guide* of all is yourself. How many times do we stand back and watch ourselves scream out in anger or come apart at the seams. At such times we watch in wonder and awe at the dramatic representation of our feelings. We certainly haven't split in two at such moments. We are, instead, experiencing two different facets of ourselves at once. The more we grow, the more aware we are of these different facets of the self. We can use them to create better frameworks for judgment. There are facets of ourselves that we cannot even relate to from the confines of this universe, although we do draw strength from them.

There are any number of ways we can respond to an event, situation or communication. We are constantly deciding which one to choose. Sometimes we become lazy and simply switch on a facet of ourselves that has become habitual or which our friends and associates have come to expect from us. As time goes on, this facet of ourselves actually becomes a part of our "personality." Because others are uncomfortable when we fail to respond as expected, we continue, forgetting we have a choice.

From time to time, because we are constantly changing and evolving, we will drop certain facets of ourselves and adopt or utilize others. When this happens, people say we have changed and so we have, although the old familiar facet still exists underneath.

Let's look back at the facet of ourselves that stood by and watched the dramatic part of ourselves. It is **this** facet that is most nearly the self we are trying to find when we are trying to **find** ourselves. It is this self that we are trying to develop now.

Keep in mind that we are still one self — but one self with many facets similar to a diamond. The light plays on each facet in turn as it moves, yet it is impossible to see all facets at once with equal light reflection from each one. And then there are the reflections of reflections that are perceived within the depth of the stone and these are constantly changing in color and intensity as the light changes.

So just as all the possibilities of light and reflections of light cannot be seen in a cut diamond all at once, so all facets of ourselves cannot be perceived or expressed all at once. Add to that, the facets of ourselves that come into being only in relation to a specialized universe or dimension, much as different aspects of our personality, may never come into being at all because there is no impetus to bring them to life. We haven't even begun to tap all the possibilities of our own personalities and *beingnesses.*

For instance, a father who gently soothes a hurt child is the same man who can squeeze through traffic in an effort to be first, is the same man who quakes in front of the boss. Each of these is the same entity but different facets of that entity.

Few of us are called upon to serve in a lifesaving capacity. Jumping into the icy lake to save one who is drowning, pulling someone out of a wrecked car just before it explodes into flames, saving a child from an onrushing vehicle — such experiences can be lifechanging. They can stir emotions and thoughts to new heights of excitement from which it is difficult to move.

Old soldiers are constantly reliving exciting, death-defying moments in an effort to again attain the altered states that lifted them from the almost two-dimensional pages of their everyday existences.

To try to accurately describe multidimensional realities in physical universe terms is as impossible as accurately describing the color blue to one who is blind from birth . . . Yet we can begin to understand on telepathic levels the more we read and look and perceive the realities of others.

The facets of ourselves that are actually evoked by the nature of this universe would not be evoked elsewhere. This is the only universe that calls your personality, as it is, into being. That is why we can grow in ways here that we cannot grow elsewhere. That is why our stay here is valuable. When we graduate from this universe we have added greatly to our store of understanding and ability and wonderful experience.

We call upon some facet of our being with which to experience and respond to whatever situation we find ourselves. We actually **decide** whether to take umbrage at a remark or simply to see it for what it is and grant rightness to it on some level. We actually **decide** whether or not to become upset over an event or whether to take it in stride and simply allow the event to take place without investing much psychic or emotional energy into it.

These decisions may not always be consciously perceived, but with awareness we sometimes become **painfully** aware of our choices.

Once We Know, We Can Never Again Not Know

It is difficult or near impossible to hide realizations from ourselves once they occur. Imagine living underground and being told that there was nothing else and one day you find a crawl space. Making your way to the top, you come to a hatchway and upon opening it you see a blue sky, grass and trees. You quickly close the hatch and return to your home underground. All the way you are arguing with yourself as to the validity of your experience, and by the time you get home you have half-convinced yourself that it was an illusion. All the same, you are forever changed by the experience. Your realities from that time on have opened up and can never again be closed.

In like manner, once you have experienced an altered state or have had a great realization, you can never go back to the same level of unawareness again.

We use our growth and awarenesses as stepping stones to even greater heights of experience and evolvement. And even if we feel cut off from our spiritual growth and find ourselves looking again through a veil, all we need to do is be patient. Nothing is lost. There is just more to see and it only **appears** as though our awareness has left us.

Our Natural Connection with the Spirit World

Our natural connection with the *spirit world* is sometimes not easy to comprehend. We enter it in thought many times, especially noble thought, and we enter it in our sleep state. Our entire essence is that of the spirit. In fact, we never **leave** the *spirit world* except through altered states, and then we become convinced the altered state is real and the *spirit world*, we think, is reached through these lower altered states.

We have interchange with the *spirit world* when we daydream and when we carry on imaginary conversations with others. It is from this world that the *third dimension* (which includes this entire physical plane) seeks and receives its creation. Without the concourse with the spiritual dimensions there would be no creation possible in the physical world. Even the raw materials with which we create the solid world have genesis in spiritual *beingness*. The tiny particles with which our world is built are made up of *beingness* — sentient *beingness*.

To deny the *spirit world* is to deny one's own *beingness*. . .one's own existence. . .one's own reality. To deny one's own imagination and the scope of one's own realities serves only to postpone one's own awakening. Also to deny the spirituality of others, the reality of the existence of others — whether in or out of the body — is again denying one's own spiritual possibilities.

We Respond to the Awakening of Others

One lovely truth, however is that we cannot deny our realities forever, and sooner or later we all have to awaken. The invitation is so great, the magnetic pull toward our own inner realities is so great and our own desirings to know are so great that we cannot cling to our own fantasies forever. They begin to fade more and more quickly as other *beings* begin to awaken. We cannot help but respond eventually to the awakenings of those around us. We find we can no longer hold on to old ideas as we see other proofs bombarding us every day at every turn.

We finally discover we are a part of *All There Is* — earth, wind, fire, all physical creations (trees, rocks, mountains the fish in the sea, the birds flying free, the colors of the sunrise and sunset, the evening star, the waterfall, the air we breathe, even our bodies throughout all their cycles and ages) all emotions and experiences, all particles of existence, all *beings* everywhere, all dimensions, all thought, all creation, all imagination, God — *All There Is*.

> All we have thought of as adventure in this world pales beside the most exciting adventure of all: our return to *Real Reality*.

In truth, the *spirit world* exists everywhere, even in the physical universe. It is always "here," never "there," so in order to find it, we look within to that beautiful, personal universe that is ours. That is where we find *Real Reality*. That is where we communicate with our *guides* and *friends*. That is where we find our own *inner beingness* and *knowingness*. That is where we connect again with *All There Is*.

CHAPTER FIVE

THE NATURE OF COMMUNICATION WITH SPIRIT GUIDES

Once you are reintroduced to your *guides*, either by your own recognition or through the help of one who can communicate with your *guides* for you, you are then free to communicate on your own and become reacquainted. Because the interchange is so close and personal it may seem as though you are "making it up." The truth is, we are a **part** of all the communication we receive. It is not coming from the vast everywhere — from strange and unknowable sources. It is also coming from **within** and that may feel as though it is our own voice we hear. Sometimes it is but it can be trusted every bit as much as a voice from another. We **can** trust our own *inner beingness*. As long as we understand that the communication is not coming from outside us — from the physical universe — it is easier to comprehend.

To get the concept of our bodies being a "window," so to speak, into other dimensions, as well as all we can see or perceive of the physical universe, helps us get the idea of **where** the communications are coming from. As we have noted before, **where** is **here**. Not off somewhere else.

Now, *All There Is* exists **within** us. No matter where we go or how we perceive a world around us, *All There Is* and all we **are** exists within us. Even this physical universe exists within us and we play the game of **externalizing** it.

Who Our Guides Are

In order to be more comfortable with our *guides*, it is a good idea to know who they are. First of all, they are entities, *beings*, *spirits* who are just like you. They have, more than likely, spent time in this universe and are familiar with it. They no longer respond to life from the viewpoint of being in the physical universe but they are sensitive to our lives, our problems, our goals, because they have agreed to play the game with us as *friends* and advisers. They may communicate to us via a past personality and a name to go with it, but they do that for our convenience, not because they are still creating that personality. Sometimes they choose a personality from a past life in which you knew them and sometimes they choose their own favorite past life. It makes it easier for us to communicate with them when they actually can come through as a personality.

There are factors which govern our *beingnesses* that make it easy to recognize one another. We can sense or feel a presence that is familiar and we learn to recognize it. Those who are blind are able to develop a sensitivity that makes it possible to recognize unique vibrations of those who come around often. They can many times tell who is in the room before words are spoken. There are other aspects of recognition such as footsteps, breathing, smells, but they are also recognizing the vibration unique to that *being*. On other planes it is not necessary to be recognized by a name because we recognize each other as *beings*. When you start *channeling* your *guides* you will recognize them in the same way. You will **know** to whom you speak.

Your *guides* and others are *friends* of yours — *friends* that you have known possibly for all time. Some are newer *friends*. They are co-creating your present existence with you, along preagreed-upon lines, purposes and goals. They have great influence upon you and what you do, and they are sensitive to your problems as well as your successes. They never, never, never, however, give advice that would hamper another *being*. They love all beings and do not exercise favoritism, even though they are your special *friends*.

Our *spirit friends* are not operating in the same framework as we are. They are communicating to us from states of consciousness that are not a part of the *physical universe trance state*. Although they are not "above" us in any way, they are not playing the same *games* we are playing. Because they aren't, they can advise us from a totally objective point of view. When we leave this plane and return

Home, we will have let go of the *physical universe trance state* along with all the games, considerations, attitudes, emotions and physical "realities" that we employed in order to involve ourselves with the physical plane. All judgmentalism, criticisms and opinions are no longer a part of our thoughts when we cast off the physical world.

This is why we know when we are speaking with our *spirit friends* or with *beings* who are still involving themselves with the physical plane. Sometimes we "filter" or allow our own bias or opinion to color the communications we receive from other realms. In that case we might see bias or make-wrong or even dire warnings coming through. Our *guides* **never** give us dire warnings or suggest anything that would hurt another. Their view is ultimately objective — a trait we work toward here, even through our own involvement with the physical plane. It is possible to reach great heights in this respect.

Your *guides* will never advise one to commit a crime or other such act, whether it be against you or someone else. They have the ability to see all sides at once, and their love for all is reflected in their advice. That is why we may wonder at their advice — why one answer instead of another.

How Our Guides Speak to Us

If you are expecting to hear voices with your physical ears, you may miss the real voice that is trying to come through. Your "spiritual hearing" will not develop. If you are expecting to see your *guides* with your physical eyes, you may miss the chance to develop your "spiritual eyesight."

It is not always a good idea to belabor the significance of exactly which *guide* has "spoken" or otherwise sent a message. They give us their names in order to make it easier for us or to give us confidence. Many times the communication represents a consensus or group-agreed-upon concept and almost always includes the participation of your inner self.

Our *guides* do not need to depend upon physical universe symbolization for identification. There are many subtle and very definite individual qualities, which include telepathy and wavelength or flow, that are unmistakable. For instance, if you receive a letter from someone close to you or from a long-time friend, you would perceive, telepathically, subtle messages "between the lines." The flow or wavelength that rides along with the letter will tell you if there is something wrong that is not being expressed in words or if something is purposely being withheld. You may not choose to be consciously aware of it at the time, but may in retrospect realize that you "knew" all along what the withheld communication was.

Your ability to perceive these telepathic messages is the same ability you use to recognize your *guides* individually.

Those who are blind do not have greater ability to perceive, but they do have a greater intensity of **desire** to perceive which is aroused by necessity.

A sudden conceptual idea, a sense that everything will be all right, an unexpected spurt of self-confidence, a very real impetus toward going ahead on an idea that was abandoned — all these very probably are direct communications.

There are **many** instances in which we are encouraged, inspired or even challenged to go ahead with actions or, hold off on an action for a more advantageous opening.

"Windows" of Opportunity

Just as there are "windows," consisting of time, space and orbit position in which a rocket can be successfully launched, there are "openings" or "windows" which will more easily accept our *thought-projections* and can most easily become a reality on this plane. We speak of an "idea whose time has come" and "being at the right place at the right time." These are very real concepts and are not governed by luck or chance.

We can let these opportunities pass without taking advantage of them. The "window" rarely opens the same way twice. This does not mean that there will be no more "openings" but that they will differ because all the factors will differ from one time to another. They will also differ in length, intensity and ease of entry.

We must realize that when we put out a telepathic communication, it hangs in the air, so to speak, until the recipient is ready to receive it.

When we hear of someone dying, we can put out communication of comfort and reassurance that their *guides* are there to aid them and when the *being* is ready, the communication will be received and the *being* will know who sent it.

Our *guides* are constantly putting out communications that we may not be ready for yet but will receive when we open our windows to it. This is why there seems to be so much communication coming through when we finally do open up.

This does not mean that the information is stale or dated. Because there is no time outside the physical planes, the communication is always happening in **our** present.

The important thing to realize here is that we create our own "windows." We put out our intentions in such a way that we **know** they are real and are already happening. The plan for the "window" is made and when all other factors that go into creating that desire come together, the "window" opens.

Imagine the complex and exciting event of a window finally opening up for masses of people and whole countries and continents.

Such windows are opening wider and wider now, and that is why whole societies are becoming more spiritually aware.

As we become more aware, we have need for more expanded experience and we tend to communicate further and further across dimensions, and our worlds change as a result.

Many times, you will get whispers of enlightenment and come upon "realizations" quite independently of a present-time activity. Your *friends* have found an opportunity to communicate with you at that moment. They are whispering answers to questions you have been asking yourself.

"Bright Ideas" often come from our *friends*, whether we are consciously aware of their presence or not. This is a way in which they can share in and enhance your progress in your game. This is not to say that you can't come upon a bright idea on your own or have a sudden flash of enlightenment that is totally yours. It is merely one other way in which your *guides* can be of service to you. Remember that you are a part of **everything**, and that includes communication that comes from your *friends*. Many times, advices will reflect a consensus of opinion that also includes your inner self.

Other Beings Who Wish to Communicate

Now, since you are not "locked in" to one *family* or group, there will be times that others may want to communicate with you. It may be an old *friend* from some existence or another, an old lover or even someone for whom you were a parent. Sometimes an old business partner will pop up. Perhaps even an old admirer that you only barely noticed. These communications can be very enriching and fun. However, if you do not wish to communicate, you do not have to. If the timing is difficult — coming in the middle of a project, on the freeway or even in the bathroom — simply tell them so. (They rarely notice what you are doing when they swoop in.) You can tell them that you had rather communicate at a more convenient time, or tell them that you are tired, if you are. It is perfectly understood by those who have had concourse with physical existence, and "feelings" do not get hurt. Be sensitive, however, to the fact that any harshness to one such *being* can create problems in all other communications.

Etiquette and Attitudes toward Our Guides

Attitudes are very important and all *beings* are affected by them. To fail to acknowledge a being's presence or to fail to thank an entity for care, concern and advice is to play the part of an ingrate. There are very definite points of etiquette (for lack of a better word) that we can learn in regard to our *spirit friends*.

Our *friends* speak to us out of love and regard and it is important to respond in like kind. One can be forgiven for going to sleep during a communication because more than likely the conversation will continue while the body sleeps. It is during sleep that we do most of our communicating anyway. But to receive excellent advice and flow from a *being* or *beings* and then to walk away, so to speak, without a thank you or a sign that you are pleased is to act irresponsibly. It is comfortable to think of them as our best *friends* — just as we feel about best friends on this plane, or even more positively, and act accordingly. That includes laughter and joking around with them as well. They love it when we are not too serious.

All emotions have validity. No emotion is "wrong." When you are talking with your *friends* and are experiencing an unpleasant emotion, don't be afraid to let it out. You will never find a safer harbor in a storm than with your *guides*. They understand that all emotions are a part of the experience you are having here. They also understand that there are no **bad** emotions. If you become angry while communicating with your *friends*, rest assured that they will understand the context from which it comes.

On the other hand, to become angry for your *friends'* failure to answer as you would wish or for failure to heal you of a sickness or other problems is to be angry with yourself. They realize this. However, it is not a good idea to let yourself go in that manner. When this occurs, don't forget to communicate that you realize what has happened and to treat your *friends* as you would love yourself to be treated. You may later feel there are barriers to communicating with them, but if there are, they are of **your** making. Not theirs. They are always there. Always constant and always loving.

What We Can Expect of Our Guides

It is important that you know what you can and cannot expect of your *guides*. First of all, they will not move mountains for you. They are not likely to remove a mole from your cheek and they will not go counter to your own subconscious desires and plans in your game. They will not swoop down and save you from the consequences of a detail in your game that you have set up. Just because the going gets rough and you decide to change your mind and not go through with something you have set up, but perhaps do not know consciously that you have, will not change the fact that your *friends* are waiting for you to complete the cycle. They will not interrupt it on a whim.

In other words, imagine that through a series of events and decisions you have set it up that you will have an accident on the beach. Just before it happens, you change your mind. Your *friends* will not help you avoid the accident just because you changed your mind. Your *friends* will not desert you spiritually, however. Get the idea? If they did save us every time we got into trouble and wouldn't let us get hurt, imagine how frustrated we would become. It would be worse than having doting parents who never let us out of their sight or never let us try anything that might hurt us. Life would become untenable and we would never grow or have a chance to experiment. It is not their purpose to do "all" for you. The reason for this is clear. You came here to play a game or games, and those games include adventure, problems, danger and interesting developments. Without these you would not enjoy your existence here. All your power would have been taken away from you and you would never get the chance to realize your own *beingness*.

With these realities we can put the existence of our *spirit guides* and their involvement in our games into perspective. First of all, they are a part of the *Real Reality*, and their link with you is important in making it easier for you to see beyond the physical.

The main and most important service of our *guides* is in helping us open our awarenesses of our *inner being* and of other dimensions and other existences — not to make the physical world easier for us.

The richness of life depends upon this awareness. Physical comfort and riches on this plane will not bring about contentment and feeling of accomplishment that one might expect, but multidimensional awareness will.

Many of your *guides* have lived lives on this plane, and they have gone through many of the trials you have gone through and are going through now. They are also growing through their involvement with your physical existence. They are jubilant when you win and they win right along with you. You can do well to make this clear in your mind — that you do not let them down when you think you have lost a point or two. You haven't. We win even when we seem to lose. We win in so many ways: in the way we respond, in using the experience for growth, in weathering the experience itself and in the ways we influence others during our trials.

What we get from our *guides* is what we look for from other people on this plane. We grow up, expecting certain things from the physical universe. We are born, many times, thinking our parents are *spirit guides,* and go through entire lives being disappointed that it isn't so.

Try to imagine someone with a great deal of influence upon your life, totally dedicated to aiding in your own purposes and drives without making judgments or critiques on your performance. Imagine, if you will, a person or persons who totally understand you and your motives, desires, aspirations and goals. Imagine the softest kind of advice that carries with it no force or coercion, advice that you have total freedom to accept or not accept. Imagine a font of help and advice that never runs dry, no matter how often you decide not to take it.

It is important to note that you will not receive negative or judgmental communications from your *guides* and *friends.* If there is one really beautiful trait which belongs to all our *guides*, it is that they are completely nonjudgmental and are ready to recognize the **true** motives of you and yours. You are much more likely to judge yourself than they are to judge you. Their communication will always be of a positive and supportive nature, even if there is a refusal to answer questions.

We find that once in a while a *guide, friend* or *teacher* will cause little things to happen that delight us. Although they will ordinarily not do **big** things to clear the way for us, they can be known to do **little** things — such as making something come out just right; perhaps we find that something we thought was broken really isn't broken; even typing errors have been changed. Perhaps we thought something was lost and we look and there it is! We may find money in our pockets that we have "forgotten" was there. We may find openings in the traffic that amaze us or a surprisingly convenient parking place or other such opportunity. All such instances aren't caused by our *guides*, but many of them are. If you think so, tip your hat or otherwise acknowledge the deed. You don't need to go into great significance on it, or try to find out exactly **who** did it. You aren't expected to.

The thing to realize is that we are not to wait around and do nothing, expecting the *guides* to smooth the way for us. The job of living is ours and we are the ones who must make things happen. It is when we are doing this that our *friends* are most likely to help.

On the other hand, we know that **anything** can happen and often does. There are no limits to the experiences we can share if we are open to the possibilities. **Share** is a key word here because just as in telepathic communication, we are also a part of the good things that come to us from our *friends*.

It is important to understand that our *guides* are not at all demanding and that they are not laying great plans for us, ordering our lives. **We** make our lives happen. **We** make the decisions. **We** are the creators of our own experiences. We orchestrate our own growth and realities.

Negative Communications

If you receive any communication which is other than positive and affirming, it will be glaringly evident that someone else is playing a joke on you and has entered the *channel* which has been set up for receiving. Do not let this discourage you and by all means do not accept any of these negative remarks as truth. Most negative thoughts we have about ourselves come from this-world social standards which are best dispensed with as nontruth. In fact, **all** thoughts which tend to put us down or make us feel less have no actual basis in *Reality*. To the extent we "buy" or accept such data, we hold ourselves back and stunt our own growth. With greater understanding, we gain greater levels of ethical responsibility and that includes ethical responsibility for ourselves and our own advancement.

We Are All Doing Our Best

In truth, all of us feel we are doing what is best in the context of the game or of a detail in the game. Some may have less understanding and grasp of reality than others, but we are all certain we are in the right. When a *being* does something which he thinks to be wrong, you can be sure there is suffering involved. We tend to make ourselves pay for such acts. No one else does it. We are the judges and juries of our own actions and we mete out the punishments, if any. We are also sparse with the rewards. Humankind tends to be too hard on itself.

A point that needs to be made here is that our *friends* never **offer** advice. It comes when we ask for it. We are always free to take it or not. Their advice is not given as prophecy or pat answers from the "future." It reflects a course that will be most conducive to our fulfilling certain game plans. It does **not** reflect the **only** answer either. Sometimes our *friends* merely reflect an alternative that we have not even considered. This can lead to more creative steps being taken than would possibly otherwise have been noticed.

There are situations in which we find ourselves and instead of taking the path offered by our *friends*, we go ahead and learn a lesson all over again. This happens often. When we finally discover we really did not need to learn that particular lesson more than once, we can shrug our shoulders, laugh and go on. It isn't a matter of our *guides* being "right" — only more objective, as mentioned earlier.

Even if your *guides* suggest areas of improvements or changes they would like to see you make, they will not fault you later if you decide not to take the advice. So do not let those instances keep you from being totally open and free with them. Their suggestions are not orders but reflect views from where they are looking. They are totally willing to have you take the advice or not, because the advice represents only one probable course of action at a time. If you decide to take another course of action, then their advices will quickly begin to reflect the new direction you have taken. There are no wrong decisions. There are equally interesting developments from each possibility.

Independence and Sharing

It is important to note that you do not have to seek advice on **everything** you do. The less dependent you are upon your *guides*, the more advancement you will be making on your own. Communicating and sharing with them, however, does not mean you are dependent. Trying to get them to direct your every move is another thing entirely. They love to be requested to help, but they will not give advice that would take away from your own determination or from important game points you can make during a trying period. Do not expect them to. Sometimes it is good to merely converse with them as *friends*, sharing feelings and impressions with them. This helps bring them closer to you and you eventually find you are sharing more and more and are becoming more and more in tune with your own inner *knowingness*. They enjoy these times as much as you do. They are first and foremost *friends* in the largest sense and the more you are able to view them as such, the more enriched your stay in this world can be. The more comfortable you become with their "presences," the easier it is to be aware of other dimensions; and as you become aware of other dimensions, your growth will become stronger and "faster." Just remember, your *guide* is not a genie, bound to grant your every wish.

Interdimensional Awareness

There are ways in which you can live on this plane and be aware of many other realities and, in doing so, enrich your existence here. It is only that most *beings* have become so enamored of this dimension that they are no longer able to open up to other realities. Indeed, they are convinced that this world is all there is. This was not always so. There have been many "times" in which *beings* took for granted the ebb and flow of other worlds and dimensions. They were able to "see" parts of them and utilize the power that is opened to one who "sees."

All through the ages there have been those who could "see." They were always thought to be strange. How interesting. "Seeing" or using altered states **is** the natural state. **Not** being able to "see" is what is unnatural. Humankind has forgotten its own heritage. In order to focus on the physical reality on this plane we go into a *deep trance state*. Without it this world would have no reality for us. The *physical universe trance state* enables us to play games in physical form. it was not planned that we would totally forget our beginnings. Growing to use the best of both worlds is what will bring "heaven on Earth."

This Renascence of Awareness

In this dawning new age — this renascence of spiritual awareness — we will see wondrous things; wondrous times in which great crowds of people will be singing the praises of *astral travel*, ESP, telepathy and all the wonderful things we will be doing. These talents and abilities will be praised, not feared, as in the past. Our power will finally be understood for what it is: **the power to** — not the **power over**. Humankind will cease to be afraid on its **own** power. The pure power of life and love.

This renascence has actually begun. There are many *beings* now that have edged into greater awareness just in the last few years. More and more books are being sold on spiritual subjects. We are coming out of the old spine-tingling stage of shivering over the possibilities of the existence of ghosts or mental telepathy. We are growing up and seeing spirituality a much deeper and more meaningful pursuit.

We Cannot Look to the Physical Universe for Spiritual Confirmation

Another point is that you must not expect your *guides* to physically appear. As long as we insist upon this-world manifestations of other-world existences, we will greatly inhibit our ability to "see" into other dimensions. We must flex our abilities and extrasensory muscles in order to more fully grasp the import of other dimensions. If we can suspend our this-world symbolic dependency to any degree at all, we are on our way to freedom as individuals.

If you can "see" yourself, no matter how wispy, sitting at the table at breakfast time, you can "see" your *guides*. If you can see any recent scene as a memory, you can "see" your *spirit friends*. You can see other aspects of *Real Reality* as well. The very best, however, is to allow yourself to simply **know** they are there. What we can **know** is closer to *Real Reality* than what we can "see." The more developed and expanded we become, the less we will even reach for any other manifestation than our own **knowing**.

On the other hand, we are not saying that you will not see your *guides* or others materialize. You may indeed. What we **are** saying is that you must not think, because you don't see them in the flesh, or at least in some physical form, that you have not communicated. You are communicating to them all the time on a supraconscious level. What you want to do, we are certain, is to communicate to them **consciously**. There is absolutely nothing wrong with wanting to see manifestations as long as we realize that they will not further our growth. The more we look with our ethereal selves, the better our understanding will grow. To expect to see, with a body's physical eyes, those things which can only be perceived **outside** the confines of this universe is to miss the point entirely.

Awareness Comes When a Being Is Ready

This brings us to another point. It's best we not try to "prove" the existence of our *guides* or other *spirits* to those who are not ready to "know" that they exist. The best way is to get them to read a book which may spark a memory of their own personal universe that lies in, around and outside this universe. But to try to convince someone who is not ready is a fool's trip and can only lead to sorrow and disappointment.

Until a *being* is ready, there is **nothing** anyone can do except **suggest**. Each of us must travel our own road. We **can** be inspired by our earthly friends and many times are. So have a good book handy to give as a gift or loan to one who may need a little inspiration in order to be "ready." We can't do it by force or by making them wrong or by being condescending. It just doesn't work. It only serves to hold them back with walls of resistance.

Just because people aren't "ready" to look further than this universe for answers doesn't mean they are far behind. It may simply mean that for a period of time, for purposes of a specific kind of growth, it is necessary for them to work "alone." If that is the case, then when they are ready, they will go lightning fast to catch up. Trying to figure someone else out is difficult indeed and best left alone.

Ways of Communicating with Our Guides

Even though we describe various ways of communicating with *spirits*, your experience will be unique. There are several major ways in which we can communicate, but these are not by any means the only ones. We repeat: there is nothing cut and dried about the *spirit world*. These are not listed in order of preference or by any qualitative judgment of which is best:

1. Directly, by telepathy. It comes through as thought and "feels" mostly as though it is our own. The minute we get a surprising bit of data, we know for certain it isn't coming from us. This one needs practicing and good old-fashioned certainty. It may come as though it is a memory and may be that shadowy, but it can be trusted. One is in a light trance here. We call it "open" *channeling* or conversational *channeling*.

2. Writing or automatic writing. We can sit with pen and paper, thinking or writing down a question. Words will **instantly** come to mind. Do not "throw them away" but write them down. Trust them. Allow yourself to get over any feeling of self-consciousness. Let come what comes. Eventually, you will find yourself writing faster than you could compose sentences in your own mind.

   Do not bother to evaluate what is coming to you. This will stop the flow and is an invitation to filter. The hardest answers to write down are those that fit what we thought the answer might be or what we thought it should be; or if the answers flatter us, we tend to discount them as wishful thinking. You can rest assured that such is not the case. We, as a species, tend to disavow good things said about us or to us about ourselves.

3. *Channeling* through deeper trance. You can open yourself up and allow communication to come through, using your own body as a vehicle for the *guide*. Many times a *guide* will use the name and some aspects of personality very similar to the last physical existence or, in some cases, a favorite one. Beings are not really gender-oriented when out of physical form, although they will generally project themselves as though they are male or female.

   Some mediums are conscious of the messages coming through and some go into deeper trance states for fear of filtering or shedding bias on the messages being received. Most mediums or *channels* are careful to a fault to communicate **exactly** what is being transmitted.

There are degrees of *channeling* in this manner. It varies from light trance in which the channel's own voice and accent is used, to deep trance states in which the *guide* speaks with a totally different sound and accent. And, of course, all possible degrees that exist between. If you allow a *being* to speak, using your body to do so, the voice, accent and type of language will probably be different (even if barely perceptible) from yours. This is true, especially in deeper trance states. It can also be true if you are *channeling* while still in a conscious state. You can "listen in," so to speak. You can understand, however, that you are still a part of the communication even while in deep trance. We call this "direct" *channeling*. The *spirits* come through directly as themselves. (Many call this transmediumship, or transchanneling.)

> We are not empty shells. But you can also realize that the part of you that enters itself into the communication is your finest, most impartial self. Trust it.

That also takes practice. Your *guides* depend upon your vocabulary and your understanding while *channeling* through you, so don't be surprised to hear colloquial phrases and expressions from time to time. This does not indicate negative "filtering" at all.

4. In dreams. We communicate with our *guides* and others every time we sleep. We can learn to be conscious of this communication and to decipher our dreams. We can go to bed and establish firmly, with concentration, those things about which we wish to be enlightened. Then, while we are out of the body and are freely conversing with our *friends*, we can "work" on ideas and concepts that we want to know more about or that we want to unravel. Our dreams, however, when we can remember them, come cloaked in the symbols of this universe. Most of the time we can figure them out.

One thing for certain, others will probably not be able to figure them out for us, since symbols are mostly personal choices. Our *guides* can help us, however. They can help us be inspired by our dreams. The reason others find it difficult to translate our dreams is that a river, for instance, may signify great freedom for one person and a fear of death to another. Sometimes the "obvious" is not always true.

5. As we said before, there are other ways in which we communicate but once we open up to any of those ways, we can open up to the others. We can channel music, poetry, songs, dance, painting, drawing, architecture, design — anything at all. We can channel it by inspiration or directly allowing ourselves to surrender to another's direction, thus sharing in the creation.

6. Sharing. After having successfully channeled our *friends* for a good long period of time, we will notice that we are sharing conceptual thought and telepathic understanding without employing the usual methods of communication. This is a very high level of communication and greatly desired among our *friends*. When this happens, it signals success in reaching closely into our *inner being,* our inner knowing. The time for seeking advice is nearing an end, and *channeling* from your own *inner being* has expanded, opened a new way of expanding the awareness.

> Awareness expands to the degree we are able to connect with our inner *beingness.*

Being able to trust our own *knowingness* is vital to our growth. When we are *channeling* from our *inner being* we are tapped into *All There Is.* (This does not mean we are finished with our guides. They are closer than ever at this point).

7. Visionary communication. It does occur. We can develop the ability to see physical manifestations of *beings* — if they are indeed there. There are beings who are highly evolved enough and interested in this physical universe enough to show themselves in some kind of physical form. Failure to see one does in no way lessen the other forms of communication. We stress this because there are many who are innocently ignoring great and wondrous communications only because they cannot "see" anything. We really do not need to depend upon the physical universe to reassure us that the *spirit world* exists. We can simply "know" that it does. It needs no physical universe proof of its existence. The painting does not have to "prove" that it was created by something outside itself. It also doesn't have to "prove" that it takes something or someone outside itself to realize that it exists — yet it is true. Those who need such "proof" of the existence of the *spirit* and *beings* without bodies who can communicate with us are not ready to "know," and no amount of reasoning will convince them. It is futile to try. It is true that only those who are ready to "know"

have experienced visionary communications. Remember that true **vision** comes with understanding, not in seeing with the eyes.

Many children come into this world with the ability to "see." This will be more prevalent in the near future and their abilities will not fade as they grow older. Many babies being born now are born fully awakened and need recognition and support. They fall prey, however, to the same pressures as everyone else. They are not necessarily "perfect" babies — but their special qualities are evident early.

It is a good idea to practice various ways of communicating. There may be ways you have thought of that have not been mentioned here. All the better. Do not limit yourself to what someone else has done. Act with abandon and throw caution to the winds. By all means, do not be critical of yourself if you are unable to communicate as you wish. Be patient and use the exercises at the end of the book. They are geared to loosen you up. Anybody who is nervous or tense or too serious will have a tough time. Loosen up, relax and enjoy consciously what you have been enjoying supraconsciously all these years.

Communication with Our Guides Is Beautiful

Our communication with our *guides* is as beautiful as gold and many times as precious. There is a beauty available there that we cannot view anywhere else. That rarified world that belongs to us and our *friends* is one to cherish, love and protect. Even if we go for days, weeks, months, even years without consciously putting our attention on them, they are always there, loving us, understanding us and caring for our welfare. It is up to us to keep the passageways open. The only barriers are those we put there.

This is not an easy world in which to live and we can do well if we treat ourselves as one of the *friends*. We can do well to never forget that we are important and all that we do does make a difference — not only here but in other universes as well.

This is not to make you feel paranoid and nervous about being watched. The evaluations of what we do are not always correct when we use this-world symbols and standards with which to view them or form them. Our *friends* and *guides* are not Peeping Toms. They are much more interested in our emotional and spiritual states than in what we are reading or what we are doing in bed. Our growth does not demand of us that we become celibate, start wearing long robes and divorce ourselves from this world.

> Spirituality does not "separate" you from this world; it allows you to **connect** with *All There Is*, and that includes your life here.

You are here to play the game of life on this plane. There are a lot of ways to enjoy this world and still grow and help others grow. Perhaps the biggest challenge is to allow ourselves to relax and enjoy it.

Other Ways Our Guides Communicate with Us

There are a few more subtle ways in which our *guides* "speak" to us. They can lead us to read certain books, they can direct us to other people who will act as *channels* through which they can speak to us, they can inspire us to take trips in order to become more attuned by virtue of a change in environment, and they can lead us to places which will spark a memory or idea that will further our quest. This is not to say that every little thing that happens has a spiritual import — such as a bird flying over at a certain time. We can really get caught up in the great significance of things as some of our earlier civilizations did, but at the same time it behooves us to be alert to inspirations.

There is another point. It is not necessary to always ask questions of our *guides*. Sharing feelings and thoughts is always welcomed. It is a sign of our growth when we become aware that they are always present. We can get their attention very quickly because "time" is not involved in the process. The sooner you realize that they are a "part" of you, the sooner you will begin to relate to *All There Is*. Once you do, it will stay with you and can tap the available resources much more easily.

"Feeling"

Now, the first few times you communicate with your *guides*, you may "feel" nothing at all, but sense a certainty and knowing that you are connecting. Then again, you may "feel" physically some sort of rush of emotion, or feeling of expansion that is a little unfamiliar, or you may feel a presence or have a tingling sensation. You may have goose bumps or feel the hair on the back of your neck rise. You may even perceive and be engulfed in a flow of love. Everyone's experience is unique and what you feel one time, you may not feel the next. None of the physical manifestations are any sign that you are communicating with greater ability or power. Remember, it is a trap to think you must depend upon physical phenomena to tell you when you are being spiritually successful. To get caught up in that would be the same as asking your lamp to repair your TV set. Get the idea? We continue to mention this point because it seems to be one of the biggest stumbling blocks that stops as well as invalidates success in communicating with those in other dimensions. We cannot continue to expect the physical universe to play tricks and turn handsprings when we dip into other realms. We, certainly, can "project" physical manifestations in order to satisfy our need for certainty and many do that, thinking the materializations come from somewhere else than from themselves.

On the other hand, and there are always other hands in the matter of *Real Reality*, we must be open for bold manifestations if they do occur. Because they do. The point, we think you realize by now, is **not to expect** them to happen — not to use them as standards of whether you have successfully communicated or not.

"Seeing"

The main thing we need to do is exercise the use of our **inner eyes.** When we do, we can actually "see" parts of other dimensions. We can "see" our *spirit guides* and *friends*. We can "see" anything we want to see. Then, when we can "see," we can "know." And knowing is the very best.

When it comes to the rush of feeling in early communications, we can liken it to the feeling you had when you saw a circus for the first time, or when you saw your first shooting star. When the newness wears off, the physical sensations become much less. The surprise is gone, but not the power, beauty, truth and magic. It is the same with the existence of your *guides.* It is childish and immature to expect the rush of "feelings" each time you communicate with your *friends.* They are not producing the sensation — you are.

There may be times, however, in which your *friends* may stir the air, so to speak, in order to get your attention. They may dip into the physical universe just enough to send a "flow of love" which can very definitely be "felt" on this plane. But to think you are not connecting just because you **don't** feel anything is to put unnecessary limits upon your own powers.

Opening Up to Other Realities

There is another way in which we communicate. We can just let ourselves go and float freely, in *All There Is*, and be conscious of all we can be conscious of. Be aware of flows, waves of light and shadow, soft wisps of cloud-like formless and changing shapes — all with the eyes closed, all with the mind only. The more you do this, the more you will begin to open up. Use your imagination to conjure up all the most wonderful and beautiful sights you can — all the most beautiful and wondrous realities you can. Be ready to experience anything at all, no matter how different. This will help you break loose from all the standards of what constitutes reality on this plane.

You will begin to see dimensions within dimensions, behind dimensions, above and beneath dimensions and all occupying the same space. You will see stratified layers of consciousness. You may hear celestial music and you may even hear color and "feel" speed of motion that doesn't really move. The more we can accept other-world possibilities in our minds, the closer we come to actually bridging the gap between our own Earth-bound realities, and the endless possibilities and endless exciting worlds.

While you are floating or flying you may become aware of such levels upon and within levels of reality, all existing in the same space. When you can do this and know that it is real, you are really on your way. Now, understand that all this is in your imagination — but your imagination lives within and draws upon realities from *All There Is*.

When you can even **imagine** more than one thing occupying the same space at the same time, you can use that concept to carry you further. When we are able to go out of agreement with a few this-world laws, we leave ourselves open to all the rest that is — all that lies beyond this world.

Fearful Projections

If we are "flying" and connecting with *All There Is* and we find ourselves face to face with fearful things or monsters, just know that they are of our own construction. No one else has put them there and they have no validity beyond our own imaginations. They **are** indeed real, because everything we imagine is real; but if you know that **you** are putting them there, you can have them fade away just as easily. At any rate, they can't last long. The best way of ridding yourself of them is to face them front-on and laugh. They pop out, because they depend upon your fear to have any lasting quality. After all, it is fear that placed them there. Even if you were to perceive someone else's projection, you could make it disappear in the same manner as you would do for your own.

Communicating with Others' Guides

When we are practiced, we can "speak" with the *spirit guides* of others who are in trouble. We can be of assistance by communicating for a friend who is caught up in a confusion that doesn't seem to be resolving itself. We can follow the advices of others' *guides* in order to best assess the situation. We may be told to do nothing, in which case we must honor it. *Guides* tend to be short on advice and long on encouragement, so don't expect to have everything spelled out for you. We can work with the *spirit guides* of those who are ill and we can work as *channels* for healing flows and comfort. There are times in which this can be very valuable for all concerned.

Reverie and Daydreaming

Sometimes we sit and find ourselves not really thinking anything at all, but are in a reverie-type state. It is at these times that we are communicating on higher levels (or rather, different levels). We are in tune with *All There Is*, at least to the extent that we are able at any given point. We probably couldn't tell what is going on, because we mostly feel as though **nothing** is going on. It is at such times that we are gearing up to new realizations and our *friends* are communicating with us on a nonverbal level. We can induce that state by just sitting and "not thinking." Don't **try** not to think but let yourself just wander off in your mind. Think **lazy** if you must think anything. It is the kind of communication that children are involved in when they are just gazing out into space. Teachers could understand that a daydreaming student can catch up later and that he needs that time. It is **not** unproductive. Many learnings are taking place. Learnings and realizations that are a lot more important than memorizing the "times tables."

Daydreaming is thinking, but it is often the stepping stone to the state we describe above. . . that no-think state in which we expand and grow by recognizing other dimensions — even if we are not consciously aware that that is what we are actually doing.

Specific Advice Does Occur

While we have been strong on the concept of not expecting too much from our *guides*, let us say here that there are times that we will get very specific advice and suggestions. We may be directly inspired as to various ways of solving a problem. We may find whole plans coming into view as a result of advice from our *guides*. This kind of advice never comes, however, at times in which we are fulfilling our goals through challenges that we have set up. At these times we must realize that we are not deserted by our *friends*, but we know that they are with us, cheering us on and giving us support insofar as they can. There are goals that cannot be reached without bringing with them the challenge of our winning out against all odds — winning with only our own thrusts and energies.

We Create on Many Levels

It is difficult to realize that we are are never alone and that our winning affects many others on this plane as well as on other vibratory levels and dimensions. Meeting challenges is one of our ways of creating on more than one level — more than one world. We are so accustomed to thinking of ourselves as small and essentially incapable of the kinds of creations we are speaking of here. Our powers of creation are infinitely stronger than we have allowed ourselves to recognize.

Very little of this world is anything at all the way it seems. Our struggles to understand one another and our struggles to understand the world in which we find ourselves are all a part of the overall *universal game plan.* A plan which we all helped to devise.

Beings Seek Experience and Challenge

Every universe, world, dimension, brings with it its own field of challenges. There are very few worlds in which we simply float around and do nothing. Beings are intrinsically curious, bright, powerful, intelligent, creative, imaginative, childlike, open to adventure, loving, understanding, knowing and possess many other attributes and qualities. We are all full of the joy and celebration of our qualities as well.

We pretend to be less than we are in order to really experience this and other worlds. We want to know what it is to feel pain, anguish, fear, joy, laughter, death, life, and all the emotions we can feel along with all the gradations of each. We don't want to just see others experiencing it. We also know that in order to really experience all these things we must believe that we **can** and that we actually **are** experiencing them. We have forgotten, however, that we can feel them without being totally unmindful of *Real Reality*. But to the extent we need to know and understand emotions, problems and danger, we must suspend many aspects of our *knowingness*, otherwise deep experiences simply will not happen for us. This is why we need not feel we are stupidly going along with this universe against all reason. We do have reason to be here, playing our games. We do not, however, need to be so far away from *Real Reality* that we cannot relate to it with some confidence and *knowingness* about our true beginnings and about the possibilities open to us here. The possibilities of playing even more meaningful games, even more exciting futures and outlets, are ours in creativity. The surface has hardly been scratched in regard to the beauties, creative possibilities and wonders that could be ours even here, living as human beings in societies, co-creating great new ideas and environments.

The deeper we go into *physical universe trance states*, the fewer alternatives are open to us. Conversely, the more aware we are, the more creative we become, and with that new level of creativity come new levels of possibilities. They are endless — limitless. We limit ourselves only by becoming unaware. That is the **only** way we can limit ourselves.

Now all of this is closely connected to our *guides* and to why it is that they want to communicate. They realize the limit we have placed upon ourselves and they are willing to do all they can (short of ruining our game for us) to help us get reacquainted with *All There*

Is — and that includes the important part of becoming more and more in tune with our inner selves.

To know with certainty that there is no limit to what you can understand, know and do is to be truly happy. The old idea that there were things we had better not delve into, for fear of getting into terrible trouble, especially with the "mind," has held back more growth than all our wars put together.

You don't have to "go" anywhere or create a special event in order to experience *Real Reality*. **It happens within you.** When life becomes dull, mundane and uninteresting, then we have lost touch with *Reality*. When it sparkles, even in danger, we are creating those things in our lives that we want to have there. We are then truly in touch with *Real Reality*.

CHAPTER SIX
KINDS AND TYPES OF GUIDES

Who might we expect to contact when we reach out for our *spirit friends?* Certainly, famous and impressive personalities come to mind. How exciting to think of communicating with George Washington, Queen Elizabeth or even Socrates. Of course we can communicate with any of these — even if they are inhabiting bodies in new lives.

We communicate with the *inner being*, not necessarily the personality of one lifetime, although that personality is definitely one of the facets of the *inner being*. Whatever gains and growth experiences are garnered in one lifetime become a part of the entirety of all there is that makes up the *inner beingness*. We, then, not only benefit from a lifetime we recognize, but from all that has gone before and after. For instance, if we are communicating with George Washington, we are not merely speaking with the personality of that one lifetime, but with the knowledge, experience and wisdom that constitutes the entirety of that *beingness*. In like manner, when we contact our own *inner being* we are contacting the entirety of our own knowledge, experience and wisdom.

It is also true that we can communicate with anyone we choose. It matters not our station in life, financial status, how long we have communicated with *spirits* or how able we feel we are. Communication from the heart is always heard, understood and answered. One would not have to be a philosophical scholar, for instance, in order to give and receive communication with Socrates.

On the other hand, there are *guides* and personages who are really adept and interested in guiding who were never even mentioned in history. In fact, very few are recognizable or traceable in history.

Even if they were, it wouldn't matter. All we need are gentle nudges and loving kindness, understanding and an unbiased view from a *guide* who cares. That is most certainly what we do get from our *guides*.

There are indeed many kinds and types of *guides*. They each have their own personalities, flows, interests, talents, abilities and goals. Some of our *guides* are those who like to inspire us to mischief and laughter. They are much like jesters. The communications exist mainly for humor and fun. They do not like to be serious and they do all they can to get you to laugh at your troubles and at yourself and your condition.

Laughter

Your *guides* really enjoy it when you laugh because they come close and even enjoy the physical sensations of laughter. If they like food, they may even come close when you are eating and share in the physical sensations of tasting. These are the ones who give you silly ideas about "what would happen if I took off my clothes right in the middle of this meeting," or "wouldn't it be funny to slap the mashed potatoes across the table?" These ideas will spring to mind usually in very formal settings. Guess who are the culprits? The fact that we do not follow these suggestions but merely smile is the effect really wished for anyway. To lighten us up is a great pleasure for them.

Many humorists, comedians and clowns get very direct ideas from their *guides*. Even comic writers will. It is often that a writer may even get ideas from the *guides* of the comedian or actor. They are making sure the actor gets the "best."

Laughter is so valuable that we seem to save it up for special times, but we need to laugh as much as we can each and every day, for the sake of our health and emotional balance. If we have periods of sadness, then we must make sure we give equal time to merriment. Emotional balance is important. Conversely, if we try to spend all our time laughing, we will miss the values to be gleaned in the other emotions. That is not to say that if we have a season of laughter, there will follow without fail a terrible season of sadness. It means only that one does well not to neglect laughter and its healing properties. Healing centers in the body are naturally stimulated by laughter.

The Old and Wise

There are very old and wise *guides* who are called upon from time to time to help some *being* who needs special help. A *being* becomes "old and wise" after having evolved in a certain way, having most likely lived many lives on physical planes and learned much about them. Many *beings* have learned how to control various aspects of this universe and other physical universes. Help from them would be very expert and powerful. At this point, many are able to come closer to this plane while communicating with us than most other *guides*. Such *beings* are totally not interested in helping us out on a whim or with things we can do for ourselves.

These *guides* come from many different *families* and are not necessarily a part of the suffering *traveler's family* or group at all. They may bring people together for purposes of helping each other break loose from an excruciating situation or from a long-term unproductive period. They may even aid a *traveler* in leaving a long-dead body after years of holding on to it, not knowing what to do. Many such "lost" *beings* cannot communicate with *spirits* or *guides* because they are caught in between lower *physical universe trance states* and there is no reality there that a *spirit* even exists. Our *guides* may try to inspire us to help these unfortunate *beings* since they **can** relate to bodies. More on this subject in a later chapter.

These old, wise *guides* may sometimes aid in bringing together *beings* who have been searching for each other for long periods of time. They may bring *beings* together who have similar goals and can help one another and at the same time enrich their own experiences. They may even help with the decision of which Earth family to join for a lifetime. Our grandparents, some of them, have attempted to act as these old *guides* and many times have succeeded in supplying that comfortable feeling of having someone old and wise on our sides. Others have played that part as well.

Children

There are *guides* who love children best of all and they are often the "invisible playmates" that children insist they can see and hear. They are indeed very real and could be accepted as such. The climate of spiritual growth in an Earth family is a very precious and valuable thing and with nurturing, gentleness and love can enrich an entire life experience. Our children are also here to play a game and a big part of that game is childhood. Childhood could be a very restful and spiritually productive period of our lives.

Our children, if allowed to grow at their own speed, without pushing, will enjoy life on their own terms which is all any of us asks. **None of us wants to be pushed in order to grow**.

The Arts and Creativity

There are *guides* who inspire us in music or painting or any of the arts. There are those of us who can play an instrument without ever having taken a lesson. We call it "playing by ear." Such people are either exercising direct recall of an ability in a past life or are being directly inspired by *spirit guides*.

We can receive various intensities of inspiration. Some less direct inspirations merely help us along, while others may feed us complete artistic directions. Some may *channel* poetry or other writings. Most times they are a mixture of your creation and theirs. At any rate, whatever help you get, you are expected to take credit for it as your own, without any feeling of guilt whatsoever. After all, you have the ability to receive, and without that no creation would have occurred. You are also a great part of it, just as in any other kind of communication.

The concept of "creation" is intricate and we will attempt to communicate one facet of a reality here. All "creation" occurs as joint efforts of *beings*. Imagine those who are talented and who create beautiful effects upon us in the form of art — whether that be as a painting, sculpture, music, landscaping, architecture or any form of art that communicates a reality to others. When there are such ones, we call them artists. An artist has the ability to distill reality and communicate it in another form, that form being one which can be recognized as containing truth. You might say that an artist is a translator of truth and reality into a language that others can understand, whether or not they can articulate it in spoken words.

To go a step further, we might say the artist is a spokesman for those who can relate to a particular kind of artistic "language." Those who view, hear, or touch the art itself and who feel its communication are also a part of its "creation." **Telepathically, they have "commissioned" the artist to create the communication**. Included in the inspiration are *guides* and other *spirits* who desire to see the art being created. That is why many artists are not always appreciated at the time they are creating. Many of the *beings* who have "commissioned" the art do not come into physical form until years after its creation, if at all.

Inspiration and Expectation

We can develop our abilities to receive inspirations. Our *friends* love to be a part of an aesthetic creation — the same as we do. If we concentrate (without effort) upon receiving inspiration, it will come. Later in the book we give some exercises to help you in connecting with these inspirations and in speaking directly with your *guides*. The more you know about guides at the beginning, however, the easier it will be to communicate because you will not be expecting unreal results.

To expect physical universe signs that you have attained an altered state or have contacted another *being* or dimension is the same as asking the painting to applaud the artist. This physical dimension is such a tiny part of *All There Is* that to expect **it** to guide us or give us confirmation that other worlds exist will surely lead to a dead end. The best confirmation we can get is within our own consciousness.

We grow up expecting certain things from the physical universe. We expect things to be fair and just. We expect that if we are "good," all good things will come to us and we will be trouble free. We expect that if we gather a lot of goodies and get a big house and car and all the things that go with it, we will find security, comfort and bliss. The physical universe itself is not aware of us on that level of expectation. The burden of awareness lies within us, not within the physical universe. Just as a musical composition is not aware of you, the physical universe as and of itself is not aware of you. There are other, more complicated levels of awareness, however, which are intricate, complex and could be dealt with in a later book. For our purposes here, we can deal with the reality as described above.

We are born, thinking our parents are *spirit guides* and we go through entire lives being disappointed that it isn't so. We grow up not realizing that our parents are here, playing their own games — games that do not always include us. They are, in a sense, *spirit guides*, insofar as they are able to counsel and guide us toward better survival. But we find that we have only ourselves to turn to for counsel in order to grow and fulfill our own game plans. Some children think their parents are nothing but caretakers for them all their lives. They never see their parents as people with very real drives, abilities and goals.

Other Kinds of Inspiration

There are also daredevil *guides* who inspire us to stick our necks out, take a chance. To explore, find new vistas, travel, gamble with our very lives.

> The sweetest rewards come when we go with reckless abandon toward what we want. To wait all one's life for some future goal of adventure is to waste that life. The adventure is waiting **now**.

Don't be afraid to risk life, limb or ridicule if there is a goal you really want to achieve. Your *guides* are there to spur you on. Lay your groundwork, prepare and **go**!

The Intellect

Some of our *guides* are there to inspire us to "want to know." Many children who love to study are possibly responding to inspiration.

There are *guides* with great intellect who enjoy guiding one who loves to learn. Inquisitiveness is a trait that is best nurtured because a great many of us seem to lose that quality when job and family responsibilities surge through our lives. It can always be rehabilitated and we would do well to take advantage of each opportunity to exercise this spirit-muscle. It will help us on our way out of the solidity with which we create our barriers on this plane. That is not to say that this is a terrible place to be. Far from it. But once here, we do have the goal to get out. That is a part of the anatomy of life here. It is as though we put ourselves in a maze and play the game of finding our way out again. Of course, that isn't, by any means, the **only game** we are playing. But we do reach a point at which we no longer want to play any other game and we are then ready to stop the game of reincarnation.

Now, when we talk of intellect, we are not talking about learning the dates of all the major wars and we are not talking about knowing how to confuse others with the use of semantics. **What we are talking about is the exercising of our abilities to contact and understand our inner realities**. The exquisite experience of peering into our **own** knowledge and understanding as has been garnered throughout existence is the reward for all our travails here. For those who have forgotten it and no longer believe that it can happen or even that it exists, it will all sound "made up," but those who **have** experienced even the slightest hint of their own inner truth will go to any lengths to have more.

Healers

The idea of actually changing physical manifestations is a big one in itself. And that brings us to the subject of "healers." *Spirit guides* and others who heal are highly prized among *beings*. They possess the ability to change physical manifestations. Our own powers are limitless and we can heal ourselves as well. All *beings* can heal, but all *beings* don't use those powers. We can change our worlds on our own. We need no one else to do it for us. In fact, we create our own worlds from minute to minute. But as long as we have considerations and beliefs that are counter to the changes we want to make, we will not be healed.

For periods of time, we can sometimes suspend old beliefs that hold us back. Unless we have totally routed them out, old beliefs have the frustrating ability to descend upon us again and again. They can be sparked by an old memory or by revisiting a place in which such beliefs began.

For instance: We are grown up, but as children we suffered the indignities of being thought too insignificant to have anything of import to say. Just suppose one of us decided that he would always be insignificant so that when some trial presented itself, he got sick instead of being able to lean upon his own resources. This became a habit.

Now, a healer enters the scene. Voila! All healed. For a while the fellow is not telling himself that he is insignificant. **But** — he makes a trip home to see the family and someone laughs at an idea he presents. Before he knows it he is telling himself that he is really insignificant and he soon becomes sick again.

Now, he doesn't become sick because the family member put him down. No. He became sick because he began again to tell **himself** he was insignificant. Get the point? It isn't so much the **past** that impinges upon us, but what we are convinced of in the **present**. That which we constantly reinforce in our own minds is that which forms our futures. "I am so insignificant. I can't **believe** how insignificant I am. See what is happening around me? I can't cause anything to happen that I really want." We talk to ourselves constantly. These aren't voices from outside telling us we are no good, unworthy, insignificant, uncausing, small and weak. We don't need an outside voice. We are too busy doing it ourselves.

We are far too hard on ourselves. We have the opportunity to make of life what we want it to be and we are afraid to let it happen. We are afraid only because of the things we are constantly telling ourselves.

If we want to be healed, we must start paying attention to the things we are saying to ourselves. It is a lot of fun to search these out because we invariably laugh at how ridiculous these statements are. If we aren't able to laugh them away, it may take longer to actually get them out so they no longer have power over us. Rarely are we telling ourselves to be sick. Sickness is merely the by-product of such *thought-commands*. The creative ability that brought about the sickness is the same creative ability that also brings about health. It is our belief system and our state of mind that determines the direction of our creative abilities.

There are many reasons why a person is ill, however. Many times, the *being* needs or wants to experience physical suffering and travail in order to learn how to end it. Sometimes the *being* just hasn't learned how to focus his creative energies and makes a mistake. Much of our learning is by trial and error. But whatever the reason, when a *being* becomes cognizant of its own inner existence, then the healing can take place as old beliefs fall away. If one could totally suspend beliefs against having healing work, then healing would take place, no matter what technique was used.

Indian Guides

There are *beings* who lived lives as American Indians who at this time are desirous of being *spirit guides* for us. As a people they never grew away from the knowledge of their oneness with all life. Even parts of the Earth itself which many may consider to be dead...ground, fire, air, rocks, water and mountains — are all alive and are as intimate parts of life to these Indian *guides* as the tree, deer or human. They love this Earth and wish to be an active part of its healing. They are primarily healers, poets and singers of songs. They wish to influence us in matters of oneness with all life and the conservation, replenishment and ecology of our planet. They are ready for anyone to reach out and accept them as *guides*.

Comforting Guides

There are *beings* who are wonderful *guides* who have no form at all but they are just as real as those who play our game of shape, size and name. These are *guides* who come close to us and share with us their feelings of love, power, grace, energy and oneness. They are there to comfort and encourage us when we stumble or fall. They are there when we leave our bodies and they help us to see our way in the dark times of life in physical form.

Guides from the Fairy Plane

There are *beings* who love to play funny games with us and are similar to what we call the leprechaun, the troll, the gnome, even the fairy. They are funny, nonthreatening, light and full of love and mischief. They help us laugh and drop the seriousness that keeps us from experiencing the happiness that is available. They are different from the fun-loving *guides* mentioned earlier and they live life closer to our *third dimension* than any other of our *friends*. They live on what is described as the *fairy plane*. This plane lies just above our own top level of the *physical universe trance state* and just below the *astral plane*. They are not actually *guides* because they are also enjoying life on a type of physical plane, wafting in and out.

General Information

There are many *beings* who never serve as *guides* to our plane but do serve in a similar capacity to other planes, even other physical universes.

There are as many kinds of *guides* as you can imagine. We can even request types of *guides* to communicate with us. For instance, if we want to start a new career, say, in dancing, we could request a special *guide* that loves to inspire dancers.

There is a *guide* within your own *family* who will understand, no matter what problem you are facing at the moment. You will find that one *guide* will most probably respond to your call for help while the others stand by in the background. As we have said before, the *guide* who is most adept with your current needs will most likely be the one with whom you will be communicating. Also, one *guide* will usually be expressing a consensus of thought and the advice will reflect the collective thoughts of all your *guides* in conjunction with your own *inner beingness*.

All through your life you will find one *guide*, then another, coming to the forefront. As your life changes, so does the focus of your *friends* change. Your favorite playmate during childhood, for instance, may not be the one to guide you through marriage plans. The *guide* who helps you with your investments is probably not the one who helps you through a crisis in your Earth family.

Sometimes we share *guides* with someone else in our Earth family or with a close friend or even with a husband or wife. We do tend to gravitate toward one another. Such an alliance is rare, but does happen. Our *guides* may even have helped draw couples and groups together. Now, within this scope we will find that as individuals we are not always communicating with the same *guides* at the same time. As individuals we have different needs and preferences.

Our *guides* will never take sides in a disagreement. They leave all such things to us. They may inspire us to come to a friendly end to the argument, but one *guide* will never submit to being pitted against another. They usually laugh when we try. They know that it will be resolved.

No *guide* **belongs** to one person and not the other. Conflicts of interest simply do not exist. They are so exterior to this world that they see all the ramifications. One *guide* may inspire one of us to be more tolerant of the other or to give more credence to the ideas of another, but this is to the betterment of both.

We are totally free to speak to one another's *guides* and to any *being* whatsoever. They all respond to us equally, giving inspiration that is needed at the moment.

Contradictory Messages

If, at any time, one *guide* seems to contradict another, it will be only in the translation, not the intent as sent out by them. Also, if one person gets one message that contradicts the message someone else gets on the same subject, there are three possible reasons:

1. The questions asked were slanted differently, with slightly different inner intent, eliciting differences in response. In other words, both asked slightly different questions.
2. The different response may very well be merely one other way of looking at the problem or situation. Both are equally viable.
3. The translations are "filtered" by the individuals involved. If agreement cannot be reached, then both can *channel* a third answer, totally letting go of the original differing ones. In such cases, the third answer is invariably the best.

When you ask a question, it has inherent in it all of your life-experience and a myriad of overtones and undertones that are a part of the wavelength of vibration of your question. . .as well as your own desires in relation to the answer you would consciously and unconsciously like to receive.

Remember, you are a part of all the communication that comes to you, and the fact that it would also reflect some of your desires and opinions is natural. On top of that, the answer is reflecting the wisdom of your own *inner being* — your own inner knowing.

Eventually, after development and practice, we will find that much of the time we are *channeling* directly from our own *inner being* without the aid of our *friends*.

Now, the more we step back from our own biases and opinions while communicating with our *guides*, the more clearly we focus on the question and the more our answer reflects the *inner being* of our *guides* and ourselves. Even considering our biases and opinions, we can trust our answers while we are learning because without the guidance we are left with our biases and opinions only; so some guidance is better than no guidance. Each time you reach for answers from your *guides*, you are practicing and enlarging the opening or "window" to your own *inner being*.

Intervention from a "More Evolved" Point of View

There are many *beings* who have never taken physical form. Our *friends* communicate to them and they serve as *guides* from an even more exterior view. Their inspirations are totally spiritual in nature and they are generally quite evolved. They are conscious of us and our world, and they know what happens here but are relating to levels beyond our immediate comprehension. They, many times, are able to lend a hand to help straighten out snarls that occur when some events crash into and circumvent other events. Much as an orchestrator or choreographer will smooth out a passage so that the harmonies and movements will not cancel each other out or cause confusion, our *guides* will smooth out events that could cancel out other planned events. This does not occur frequently but there are times in which intervention is deemed necessary.

For instance: a *being* may be catapulted out of the body and become disoriented or experience such bliss that he actually forgets the body momentarily or doesn't want to come back to it. This happens most often after an accident or in surgery, and our *guides* will gently lead us back to the body and suggest that we are not finished with our games and our missions.

If our belief systems concerning death include seeing old family members, spouses, friends, religious or historically famous figures, angels or what have you, our *guides* will assume those identities for us in order to soften the shock of finding oneself in another dimension.

The *being* is encouraged to return to the body as above, and it usually works. In these cases the being is really not ready to end his relationship with his current personality.

There are other instances in which intervention occurs. *Guides* may inspire one to say something at just the right time to circumvent a possible blunder that would create a very untidy situation. In order for some events to take place, it is necessary to plan in advance, bring various components together, setting the stage, so to speak, for something to happen.

One thing to look at is that a *being* **will not** be manipulated. If a *being* is catapulted from his body in an accident or other event and **really** wants to stay out of it, no amount of coaxing will bring him back. But if he is not ready to leave the body, then it takes only a little nudge to get him to go back to it.

Nameless Guides

Most *guides*, when pressed, will make up or give a name by which they can be recognized. There are those, however, who prefer not to do so. They will not give us a name and they will not get interested in whether or not we should keep a job, or sweetheart. Their interest lies entirely in our spiritual climate, growth and enlightenment. They monitor those aspects of our lives and are really there for us when we need help, comfort and encouragement. They send love flows and acknowledgment constantly. We can lean on their love and constancy. They rarely speak to us in words but rather in conceptual thought. Their deepest desire is for us to reacquaint ourselves with our own *inner beingness.*

On other planes we are recognized by our unique *beingness* or vibration. On totally nonphysical planes we are recognized by *knowingness,* and on still other planes our oneness is so complete that any concept of separation is ludicrous although our consciousness includes consciousness of self as an individual.

Impossible to Categorize All Guides

It would be impossible to list every possible kind of *spirit guide.* They are as numerous and different as the people who inhabit this planet.

There are *beings* who only act as *guides* once in a century or so. There are *guides* whose interests lie solely in other times and ages, and so they are in a sense, focusing outside our present time frame.

There are *guides* who communicate almost exclusively during dream states and serve as *teachers* or long-standing advisers. There are those who prefer to heal us during our sleep states when our conscious barriers are lowered.

There are *beings* who have left their bodies and pretend to be *guides* at times. They are not necessarily interested in guiding you to your *inner being* but want only to enjoy the freedom of not having a body while still playing out a satisfying game of communication with us. They are not always reliable as to their advices. They may be interested in looking for gold, or playing the horses or advising you on the market. The degree of expertise will vary one from another and you can act accordingly.

Beings will fall into all possible categories and some are mentioned in detail in Chapter Eight. They are not evil but can cause confusion. They are easily handled, however.

There are *guides* who assume momentary physical form in order to communicate within this time-space-matter-energy coordinate for various reasons of their own. This is considered a very high form of communication and very probably will not happen when one is exerting great effort toward its materialization. It does happen, however, and most of the time is not recognized as being what it is.

There are realms so removed from the physical that an entity would need to extend a long "thread" through many "layers" of *Reality* in order to communicate even to our *guides*. Such descriptions of size and distance only serve to symbolically aid you in the concept of this plane. There are steps or gradations through which a *being* comes in order to assume the correct state of mind necessary to make **any** world real to him. We refer to these steps as "layers."

Due to the necessary *physical universe trance state*, certain concepts are difficult to fathom. We could look at our sonar equipment that is designed to pierce through layers of water depths to "touch" or in a sense "communicate" with possible objects on the ocean floor below.

This is similar in nature to communication from *beings* from exceedingly far-removed realms or dimensions.

Whatever form our *guides* and their communications take, they are all desirous of the same thing: our increased awareness and our reconnection with our own *inner being* and with *All There Is*. The inspiration inherent in the beautiful vibrations of their communications enlivens and energizes us to new heights of realization and experience. As we grow in awareness, the Earth-potential expands and the time of miracles becomes *Reality*.

Books such as this one are written to spark a flame into being. A flame, that once ignited, will never go out and will serve as a beacon to light the way out of the labyrinth of this world. A flame, that will lighten the darkest of corners and dead ends and gain us access to the farthest reaches of *All There Is*. You might say our **spirit guides** are the keepers of this flame and the sooner we recognize them and acknowledge their existence, the brighter this flame burns. For with their help we can truly own our own existence. We can begin to take charge as never before. We can really be safe, then, to unleash our power and creative energies — using them in ways we never before dreamed we could. Using them in ways that can change our world for the better — changing our world to fit the ideal every *being* knows and for which every *being* experiences great longing.

CHAPTER SEVEN

HOME AND THE "DEATH EXPERIENCE"

Each of us came into this universe from another universe or dimension we call *Home*. It is from *Home* that our *guides* communicate to us. When we leave our physical forms at the end of our present life cycle, we return *Home* for a period of reflection and evaluation of our life here.

All that exists is spirit, and that includes all matter, energy, space and time, all dimensions and all creation in *All There Is*. Now, when we look at the *Reality* of a *Home Universe*, we are looking at a point of view — a state of mind. We are looking at *Real Reality*. It is the same, *family* to *family*. When we return to our *Home Universe*, we are actually returning to a state of mind — a state in which we and the rest of our *spirit family* share realities and viewpoints of Life upon which we have agreed.

There is vast agreement one family to another and the reality of *Oneness* is total.

Home is where we are our total selves, our free and evolved *inner beingnesses*. When we return *Home*, we have added experience and scope to our already perfect selves. We are never "more" or "less." We do expand in awareness through experience. We might see this as a kind of "growth," though that is not a precise description since we are essentially complete beings throughout all eternity. We are complete even while being involved in realities removed from the *Home Viewpoints*.

When we leave *Home* to enter **any** other universe (state of mind), we temporarily suspend portions of the *Home Viewpoint*. This makes it possible to fully experience other viewpoints — other realities. We often leave *Home* in stages, gradually letting go of the familiar states of mind, slipping into different realities bit by bit.

For any *being* to dip into any sort of universe that is unlike *Real Reality*, he must first "forget" great portions of *Real Reality*. One must totally delude himself in order to "believe" that these physical worlds exist at all. He must steep himself in the **apparent** reality in order to play his intended game. In the case of this physical universe he accomplishes his goal through the use of the *physical universe trance states*.

If you've ever gone to a movie and become so swept up in the story and scenery that you actually felt you were there, then you have the concept of what is happening as we come into this world — this state of mind — that produces the effect of there being a solid universe and that we are here in it.

Stages of Life after Death

STAGE ONE — LEAVING THE BODY
Just as we decide upon entering a body, we also decide upon leaving it. We generally decide when we will leave it, not always **how**. On some level we do know, but not always consciously.

There is no "sensation" of leaving the body. We leave by going "inward" into our own personal worlds. If the "Death Experience" is violent or sudden, we may go further **into** the *physical universe trance states* instead of out.

Now, let's say we have a hypothetical person here who has just left her body, allowing it to die. She may not realize at first that she no longer has a body. When she does, she probably will feel so good being free of the pressures of a body and close involvement with the physical universe that she finds herself unwilling to consider returning.

If a person mistakenly thinks it is time to leave, the *guides* will gently encourage her to return to the body. This usually does happen.

If she is still very interested and anxious to return to physical form in this universe, she may not go all the way *Home* before returning to inhabit another body. In such cases, the *being* is creating her future-life scenario very quickly and may have even begun before leaving her last body.

Whatever happens, *guides* and *friends* are waiting to help her go through any confusion or disorientation that comes as a result of realization of body death.

She is cradled by her *friends* much in the same way a mother whale cradles her baby. They see to it that she does not fall into hallucinatory traps that can hold her back for long, unproductive periods. They nudge her to awaken to *Real Reality*.

STAGE TWO — COMMUNICATION AND INFLUENCE OF RELATIVES

When a *being* leaves a body, he may hover around it, seeing to it that it is treated properly. If the funeral comes within a few days, the *being* usually hangs around for that — trying to comfort the family and communicate to them. There is varying adeptness in communication between one who has left a body and those still here.

Relatives may be anxious to get messages from their loved ones. Their anxiety does nothing to comfort or make communication easier. In fact, a wait of at least six months to a year is best, giving the *being* time to come up from the lower levels of decompression. No questions or attempts to reach him with other than prayers and flows of love is the best avenue to take. After that time, communication is easier and success more assured.

Certainly, if a *being* "dies" who had led a life in which his family has had great disagreement, the thoughts and heavy opinions of the supposed state of mind and possible punishment will impinge upon the *being*. There have been instances of those who have "died" feeling so guilty that the negative thoughts of family and friends aided in his creating a "hell" for himself, thus having him caught in between dimensions on lower levels. Once one is so caught, it is extremely difficult to get out because it is the frame of mind that keeps us in any state. The "realities" of the lower depths of the *physical universe trance states* make it very difficult to realize that one can be caught in one's own "hell" or relive a *death experience* over and over and over again. It does happen, however.

The point here is that our wishes and thoughts about one who has left the body can influence his thoughts about himself. We can be of aid to one who "dies" through violence or in a state of guilt merely by prayers of love and compassion.

It is a wonderful idea to have our friends on the Earth plane share our transition period with us. It can be comforting to all involved. It also increases awareness in all participants. The transition period is delicate and is a period in which gentle thoughts and prayers are of great value and assistance. Any judgments on our parts or even constant reaching out to communicate only add problems to this sensitive period. If a *being* wishes to communicate to Earth beings sooner than six months to a year after transition, then most certainly he is ready to give and receive communication.

STAGE THREE — DECOMPRESSION

Just as we come gradually away from *Home* into this universe, we leave it gradually. Our "awakening" even now, if we look at it, has come in gradual steps. We can look back to weeks or months ago from this point and see how we have changed and grown. So we can see that our present stages of awakening on this plane are very similar to the way we continue to awaken after leaving the body.

There are rare exceptions, but most *beings* need to go *Home* in stages through a type of *decompression period* in a *chamber*, or special dimension which is still connected to and similar in some ways to this world. Otherwise, the shock is too great.

Decompression is perhaps the best way to describe how we get from the physical universe plane to *Home*. We come up through various levels or dimensions that take us gradually out of our *physical universe trance states*.

During the *decompression period*, our person may experience hallucinatory "after-death" episodes that conform with her expectations. There are, with many, such strong projections of what is expected "on the other side," that to encounter *Real Reality* would send the *being* into a tailspin that would be very hard to stop. And since she would have to stop it herself, her *guides* try to make sure that it doesn't happen. The *being* just must act out a certain scenario or portion of it before she can comprehend that there are dimensions with which she is totally familiar but has forgotten.

Her *guides* may take part in her scenario or in her expected experience. As soon as they can, they begin to introduce her bit by bit to aspects of *Real Reality*.

For all of us there is this period of *decompression* in which we get our bearings. Our *friends* are always there, seeing to our welfare but not interfering with our own powers of reorientation. There may be some "old hands" who specialize in helping those in *decompression*. They may or may not be members of our own *family* but are probably not totally unknown to us either. They act as *teachers* and *guides* who help us regroup and reorient ourselves. The period of *decompression* is different from one to another, and in Earth time can last hours or hundreds of years.

These *chambers* or levels of *decompression* have been described in many ways and there is truth in all of them. The **number** of *chambers* and time spent in each one also varies *being* to *being*. There are those who require a great number of levels to prepare them sufficiently for the concept of *Life* totally outside any sort of physical plane. This is due mostly to their having spent many lifetimes immersed in the lower depths of the *physical universe trance states*. There are gradations to these states and there are those who have lifted themselves into the higher or lighter end. They have become aware of even the possibility of other dimensions. Their experience may very well be much swifter and easier. Then there are those who are exceedingly aware and little or no *decompression period* is necessary.

ANCIENT CHANNELINGS

Ancient religions received *channeled* information concerning these *decompression* steps, allowing the Earth friends to be a part of the celebration of transition between physical life and *spirit life*. Those who were "prepared" by the information contained in these steps were able to go through them without fear.

It is not necessary at this point to seek out this ancient information. By reading this book a *being* will have had memory centers opened, whether or not there is analytical knowledge of it. Memory centers are opened for you and the transition period will have none of the fear or fearful projections that it might have had. If you hadn't before, you have now crawled up and opened the hatchway and have seen the sky. It is impossible that you could now go back into "not knowing."

It is not so much that the information in this book contains the only "truth." It doesn't. There are many truths and many *channels* for truth. But what this book **does** contain are keys to the opening of your spiritual memory centers in which you are free to sort out all information and experience that you perceive — all without having to depend upon religions or others to sort it all out for you. In the final analysis, we each have to do our own sorting out, and with our memory centers opened we are in a position to be independent while connecting with *All There Is*. In this way we can experience the *beingness* of self and the realities and connections with all of *Life* everywhere — on every level, plane or Reality. This is **freedom**.

STAGE FOUR — REORIENTATION

As we come up out of the *decompression* stages we become reoriented to *Real Reality*. Our awareness of *All There Is* grows increasingly and at last we have again attained the state of mind necessary to return *Home*.

In truth, a part of this reorientation begins for many before leaving the physical plane. Those who begin to awaken before body death are already experiencing some reconnection with *Real Reality*. It is a kind of rebirth, and even as birth on this plane is a miraculous and moving experience for all who witness it, the reawakening of a *being* who has courageously faced the strange worlds far from *Home* and finds his way back is the most moving of all experiences.

Our *guides* are very proud of us when we begin to find *Real Reality* on our own. They understand how difficult it is and realize fully the enormity of the rewards.

As we begin to reawaken to *Real Reality*, there is great peaceful excitement — a growing realization that builds and builds and culminates in a blossoming type of experience. The understanding of *All There Is* and the instant reconnection of *Oneness* and the love that emerges with passionate power is enormous and brings about great celebrations throughout your *spirit family*. It is enough to cause one to want to experience it all over again — and many times we do. From world to world, experience to experience, it is always just as wonderful coming *Home*. The old phrase "You can't go home again" is only true on this plane. Going *Home* is beautiful and there is no other experience that can compare to it.

STAGE FIVE — LIFE EVALUATION

After the period of reorientation we are ready to evaluate our just-past physical existence and tote up our "points," see our "mistakes," assess our successes and get an overall picture of our game and how we have played it. We decide whether or not we have attained the goals we set out for ourselves. It is at this point that we are able to objectively assess our games. We decide then if we want to go back and finish something we started and feel the need to finish, or whether we want to range around and observe others for a while. We may even serve as *spirit guide* to someone else, along with a few other pursuits of our own.

It is at this point that our Earth experience is fully "shared" with others.

We may decide to visit another dimension either for further challenge and growth or perhaps choose one for a vacation — a kind of rest period before going on. We may even stay at *Home* for a while, entering into group projects. The choice is always ours.

Assurance and Comfort Regarding the After-Death Experience

The more we understand and are aware before leaving a body, the more adept we will be in handling the other dimensions we encounter. One thing for sure is that we will not be alone. We are never alone. The frightening aspect of death simply does not exist unless we create it for ourselves, and even then its duration is quite short. There is nothing in *Real Reality* to aid in its perpetuation.

A wonderful thing happens when we finally **know** that our *friends* exist and are there for us. We drop old ideas about ourselves that are not true. We feel so much more the reality of ourselves and who we are. We cease being lonely and afraid of loneliness.

Even if we are not looking at it or even if we are not conscious of it, the sun rises anyway. We can depend upon it. So we can depend upon our *friends*. They are always there, whether or not we can "see" or "hear" them.

There are times in which a *being* may go immediately to other planes without waiting for the funeral and be out of active contact with Earth friends and family for long periods of time. This happens when a *being* is long overdue on ending reincarnation; is so enamored of this universe, popping right into a new body; or when he has come for only one lifetime and after leaving becomes disinterested in the physical plane and the problems concerning it.

There are those who are reluctant to leave this plane and these *physical universe trance states*. These are the ones who pop right back in. They rarely spend much time in the between-life area before returning to assume a new body and a new identity. We find this most often with groups of people who insist upon reincarnating within the same group or family.

After death, the *being*, having been convinced that he must return to a specific area, will do so without going through *decompression* or returning *Home*. There is no time of reflection — no time of rest and evaluation of the life just led. This can result in great periods of unawareness and unproductivity until the *being* finally begins to see things for himself.

All the feelings we have or would like to have about *Home* here on this plane are the feelings we have experienced about our *Home Universes*. All the warmth and welcome — all the love and understanding — all the comfort and security — and all the acceptance are there. The best part of it all is that even while here on this plane we can tap into the love and energy of our *Home Universes*. The sure knowledge of the existence of *Home* is as a quantum leap up and out of the depths of the *physical universe trance states* and into the states closer and closer to *Real Reality*. To recognize the source of our many beginnings is to come into our knowing the *Reality* of *God* and our relationship to that energy.

CHAPTER EIGHT

ALTERED STATES

Before we define **altered** states, let's take a look at the "normal" or "median" state of a human being residing on planet Earth.

We have spoken of the *physical universe trance state* as that state necessary if one wishes to be able to perceive through the five physical senses all the matter, energy, space and time that are the components of this universe. Within the *physical universe trance state* we find many levels of consciousness. We can think of these states as higher or lower, nearer or farther away. Perhaps the latter more nearly describes the reality since no state that exists is bad.

If one is playing a game that necessitates reality focused deeply into the physical universe reality, then the state of consciousness would definitely have to be "lowered" or become more remotely attuned in order for that to occur. For example, for one to experience being destroyed or blown up, one must suspend *Real Reality* (in other words, go into exceedingly deep *physical universe trance states*) almost totally in order to let self-destruction occur. The quality of the experience depends upon it.

Conversely, when one wishes to walk upon hot coals without being burned, one must suspend all lower *physical universe trance states*, coming closer to dimensions that lie next to but not beyond the edges of this third dimension.

Multilevels of the Physical Universe Trance State

We might even say, for purposes of clarification, that there are many dimensions within this one physical universe dimension and as we travel in and out of them, our reality varies. When one is depressed, it is almost impossible to admit that one could be a happy, spiritual, causative, creative and even magical person. The *gray worlds* in the lower *physical universe trance states* admit very little sunlight or positive thinking. It seems as though the reality of that state will last forever and there is no way out.

On the other hand, when one is in a high mood of exhilaration and happiness, it is impossible to really perceive being depressed. There may be a foggy memory, but the reality of it is very wispy. Great pain is felt on certain *physical universe trance levels* and not on others.

The birthing state that most mothers experience carries them into deep *physical universe trance levels* from which they quickly rise when the birth is accomplished. So quickly is great pain forgotten and great joy experienced upon first glimpse, first touch of one's newborn. It brings one out of the depths into great exhilaration. Fathers will many times experience similar states in an effort to be a real part of the birthing process. It is a sharing that when acknowledged by self and others can result in that wonderful state of joy which is just as real for him as for the mother.

Some new mothers get stuck on a level on the way up and are unable to rise higher. This is sometimes caused by the drugs that are given during the birthing or by insensitive handling by attendants and doctors. Sometimes it is caused by guilts and fears associated with the mother's own childhood. It is usually called "postpartum blues." It passes when the mother is able to finally come out of that lower state into her own usual trance state.

The pain felt during a stay on a different-than-usual trance level is forgotten when one changes levels. There are deep levels to which one can drop and recall all pains ever suffered. It is on these levels that one becomes sick and, on occasion, injured.

Now, if a person finds it difficult to appreciate beauty, music, art, etc. then there is definitely a lowered *physical universe trance level* involved. There are levels upon levels upon levels. These levels are not stacked neatly upon one another but waft in and out of one another so that one can, and usually does, view from more than one level at a time. We find that we can generally find our own most comfortable or familiar level and, depending upon how versatile we are at changing levels, we can enjoy a very wide variety of experiences and realities.

Now, because dimensions or levels of consciousness are not all neatly stacked upon one another but are interchanging in millions of ways, we will not always find ourselves responding from only one level at a time. We waft back and forth between levels and parts of levels from moment to moment as our lives unfold around us. We find ourselves responding as from one level and another depending upon the situation or subject addressed.

A young mother, for instance may be totally involved in a conversation with a *friend*, but may be on her way out the door to respond to a danger cry from a child — and may even respond seconds **before** the cry is actually heard. Get the idea? The level of awareness that makes such a quick response possible is very probably not the same level of awareness employed in gossiping about one's neighbor, or planning for a party, or canvassing for a charity.

A man who is trying to sell his boss on a new project for the company is using one level of awareness but minutes later, he may be confronted with an emergency in the mail room in which he uses a completely new set of awarenesses to solve that problem. Then, later on the way home on the freeway, his awareness level again changes.

We are wafting in and out of several stages of awareness within the scope of one day. Rarely do we have to employ a state far removed from our old familiar patterns. A catastrophe may evoke many different responses from the people caught up in it. Some will become strong and heroic. Others will become apathetic and fearful, unable to physically respond. They will sit around in a state of impotence. Others may become terrified and go into hysteria. Still others may freeze and not be able to respond at all. Then there are those who will use the bodies of others with which to climb to safety for themselves, totally negating the plight of fellow beings. Then there are those who find themselves able to comfort and help others, totally unaware of injuries to their own bodies until much later.

All these people are responding via the level of consciousness that they naturally slid into at the onset of the catastrophe. We react as we do depending upon our state of mind just prior to the event. We all have the potential for responding in all possible ways. We many times judge ourselves harshly for those things that are very difficult to control. The more aware we are at the onset of a catastrophe, the more causatively we are able to respond.

Reality Lies Concurrently
with the Trance Level

If we take this concept a step further, we could describe the state of the so-called "normal" person. The inability to even conceive of other universes or of multiple states of mind is a reality that lies on one of the *physical universe trance state* levels. Get the idea? It is not simply a matter of **telling** someone about the existence of other universes, *spirits*, trance states, reincarnation or even the concept of infinity. One must come into a different level of consciousness in order to even be able to visualize these possibilities.

THE STATE OF CHILD'S PLAY

When we become frustrated or angry at a person who is unable to understand us, simply realize that they are viewing from an entirely different point of view — such point of view being the result of the particular *physical universe trance states* from which the viewing occurs.

How many have wished they were children again so they could appreciate things from that viewpoint? We **can** experience any level, any viewpoint at any age. We have simply to find the state and go into it and there we are. Since the state of **child** takes a willingness and ability to suspend many realities and become uninhibited, it is most easily reached during hypnosis which seems to grant "permission" to suspend adult realities.

If you will recall, when playing as children, no one dared step through a "wall" or fail to open and close the imaginary "doors." It was necessary to make it "real" in order to stay in the altered state of *child's play* and when played, it is the stuff of which all our dreams, expectations, projections and futures are made.

If you look at it closely, you have to admit that the business world is constructed similarly to child's play. It would have to be so for grown men and women to be enamored by symbols such as plaques on the wall or keys to executive bathrooms.

If we could consciously use the altered state of *child's play*, we could change entire lives and existences. This state is a parody of the way we delude ourselves into the realities that make up this universe. It is terrific therapy and serves to take the seriousness out of our lives — unless we get terribly serious in our play. Adult games at parties are sometimes laced with this altered state. When there is a great good time, you can **bet** it is.

There are businessmen and women who enjoy their work so much that they live within and on the edges of the altered state of *child's play* most of the time. These are the enthusiastic and happy people who declare that they would do the job for nothing. This doesn't mean that they never have a problem or never are depressed or sad. But they, for the most part, are able to keep it light and simple. As a result, their lives are more rewarding and productive than they would be otherwise.

There are other types of delusion that appear to be *child's play* but are active delusions raised in the attempt to hide from problems and challenges. Such states are sometimes recognizable by the giddy aspect of the communication, whereas, the true *child's play* artist can instantly become serious when the situation warrants it.

The truth is, we can create any kind of altered state we wish to create. We can create any kind of **world** we wish to create and we can create any kind of effect that we can imagine. We are, first and last, **creators**. So that when we leave the body, allowing it to die, we quickly begin to organize our next experience — usually based upon expectations borrowed from some segment of society.

These experiences are *real* insofar as anything we create is *real*, but when faced with the greater *realities*, they soon fade and we finally "remember."

THE STATE OF ACTING

In a very true sense, actors playing parts on a stage are creating *real* existences — especially those who make up past histories for their characters in order to more easily create a "true-to-life" character. When a scene is acted well, even the audience knows it is *real*, and for that space in time the characters really do exist — apart and very separate from the personality that is playing the part.

For instance: suppose a scene involves a family at a dinner table. There are conversations and small events taking place; personalities are developed to fit the intent of the writer and director and actors, and it "plays" well and "works." When a scene "works," we mean it seems *real* and believable and the pace is natural and interesting. Now, during the playing of this scene, the family **really does exist!** The actors feel it, the audience feels it, the director feels it and the writer feels it. The actors experience an exquisite kind of exhilaration that may last for hours or days. The scene as played that particular night will never be forgotten and will be told as stories for years to come. That is how real it was. Sometimes, the whole play's performance will attain this "magic" aspect.

Even in sports there are similar experiences — certain "plays" are remembered and repeated as stories for years and years and referred to as comparisons to other plays in present time. These events took on "larger than life" aspects and created "magic" in our lives. And these kinds of magic are always remembered.

What is happening here is that aspirations, expectations and intentions have all come together within the entire group and the *magic* really does happen. This is what producers, directors, writers, actors, coaches and players are working toward. And when it happens, there is no experience to compare to it. The reason it doesn't always happen is that egos clash and become cross-purposed to merely creating a magic moment on stage or on film or on the playing field — and the magic rarely survives that.

There is another side to this state of acting. There are those who are pretending they are one personality and are actually another personality. These are people we may label as "phony" or even insane. Aunt Bertha, who makes the whole family uncomfortable with her flimsy pretense, and little Kevin, who acts as though the family should believe him when he says his Teddy Bear ate the cookies, are literally living in a dimension of "acting." More than likely, on some plane, they have convinced themselves of the role they are playing. The really clever ones will convince us all.

Deluding oneself is all a part of the state of mind of acting. Doing that on stage is different from doing it in life. Olivia pretends she is shy and retiring but is in reality a very strong purposeful woman. Her role seems to make her life easier than if she were to admit her strength. This is true many times of women or men who are suppressed or oppressed. They fear the fight that "always" ensues when they reveal their own power, so they submerge more and more until they are almost convinced it is true that they are weak or stupid or worse.

There are many more examples we could describe.

Moving in and out of Trance Levels

We speak to people all the time who are not in the same trance level from which we are viewing: the storekeeper, the child crossing the street, the policeman giving us a ticket, the actor on stage, our spouse at the end of a rough day, our boss who doesn't realize his own demands and we could go on and on. All these people are gliding through different trance levels — even during the day the trance level may change many times depending upon the situation.

We definitely leap into different states during times of emergency and accomplish feats that astound us in retrospect. We come out of our first trance state when we awaken from sleep. We drift for a few minutes or more until we are resigned to entering the state necessary to operate a car or enter a bus or train for work. If the mother stays home, she must enter a state in which she can depend upon herself to be responsible for her children. Many mothers can actually remember coming out of sleep or in the midst of a conversation, completely alert, running to aid a hurt child. To respond to an emergency takes a certain trance state. Some who are unable to respond quickly may become stuck in the "no action"; the *being* "freezes" and is unable to move. This trance state is frustrating and frightening to the one who is experiencing it and when others scream at them or become angry, the state persists longer because it becomes frightening and unsafe to move up and out.

It would appear that those who can move easily from one trance level to another are the ones who are experiencing the greatest variety of physical universe possibilities. On the other hand, those who are stuck are also experiencing a great number of events — mostly inside of themselves. Perhaps they want to know what it is like to experience being stuck.

Now, since all these experiences are the reasons why we are here, how can we possibly be angry with someone else just because they are in a different state from ours? How can we see them as wrong for playing the game — their game? We choose or choose not to be a part of someone's game. We are never victims no matter how it looks and we are all playing games. We are all experiencing those things we choose to experience. The trick is to be able to experience our games in a way that allows others to play games and, at the same time, hopefully connect with each other meaningfully. All this to the end of recognizing again the reality of *All There Is* and our part in it. Recognizing that we are all a part of each other. An intimate part.

"Chronic" Trance States

The trance level that contains our dearest belief systems is the level we try to keep stable for ourselves. We might call this our **chronic state**. When we see a friend who seems to believe one thing one day and changes her mind the next, we are viewing someone who is wafting in and out of trance levels. This is usually caused by confusions in the environment or great disturbances in the psyche. There are many reasons for this going back and forth. It may involve an inability to admit *knowingness* and the fear of going into "higher" states. It may involve a fear of going into "lower" states. Spiritual healings can aid such a person in stabilizing.

Understand that there is nothing **wrong** with **any** phenomena or state, and a person may very well be satisfying "karmic" involvements and probably is.

So What, Then, Is an Altered State?

An altered state is that state which takes us out of the ordinary levels within which we usually operate (our *chronic states*). For sake of clarification, say, a person operates on five general levels of consciousness during a day. Any state that takes him into "unfamiliar" territory can be considered an **altered state**. For instance, if a person is accustomed to responding to emergencies (such as a fireman or doctor) then the state necessary for handling emergencies would not "feel" unfamiliar, so would not be described as an altered state for that person — although it is. On the other hand, an office worker leaving the city at the end of the day who jumps into a river to save the life of a child will definitely experience all the phenomena of having been in an altered state.

Instances of Altered States

When we converse with our *friends* or *guides* or to any other *being* outside a body, we are using altered states with which to connect. When we daydream, we are using an altered state. When we think of something very important and work out possibilities in our minds, we are using an altered state. When we go into reverie or recall to contact a past event, we are using an altered state. When we give ourselves over to music and feel the total joy of it, we are using an altered state. These are all states from which we can take off to even deeper states, all without drugs or any other outside stimuli.

Now, if none of the above seems to be any you have experienced, all you have to do is remember the last time you were busy with a project of some kind and everything except what you were working on disappeared and you didn't even hear other sounds around you. Certain levels of concentration take us into altered states. They can prove to be very productive and creative times.

You may also have experienced a feeling of frustration and perhaps even anger when interrupted. That is due to the sudden change of viewpoint which brings you back into the body-consciousness with an uncomfortable force. We have all experienced being awakened suddenly and feeling out of sorts. Same reason.

It may be a good idea to have agreements with those who may need to interrupt such concentrations. Perhaps music of a favorite kind, played softly at first, then gradually louder until it impinges, would be a good signal that allows the body to receive you with less jolt. A whisper of your name may be another good way. It is important that those around you not be made to suffer from your "comings and goings."

How Are Altered States Induced?

THE DECISION
Since we came to this plane in order to experience all we can experience before we remember *Real Reality* and before we become aware of *All There Is*, the answer lies in the fact that we **want** to go back and forth between different states. **The decision is always the strongest factor.** Altered states can be induced by sudden realizations of a spiritual nature — inspiration from a book or lecture or even a "chance" remark overheard. Deep inside us — inside our *inner being* — lies the decision to play the game and then remember *Real Reality*. Remember our beginnings. Remember our involvement with *All There Is*. Remember that we are a part of it and that it is all a part of us.

PRACTICAL DEMONSTRATIONS
It is true that we grow through laughter. Laughter excites certain psychic centers — much as strumming a guitar or harp. One string makes all of the rest vibrate and if the vibration is strong enough, we hear overtones or sympathetic vibrations which are known to vibrate even in other dimensions. They do sound as though they are coming from "some other place."

Sit down at a piano (tuned) and while holding down the sustaining pedal, play an octave in the bass section over and over very loudly; then while still holding down the pedal, lift your hand and listen.

You should also hear a tone which is five tones higher than the one you played. Sometimes, if the piano is tuned just right, you may hear even more different tones. They do, indeed, sound ethereal as though they are coming from elsewhere. This is a practical demonstration to give you an idea of how one particle helps create another and how our own "tones" are affected by what we do.

Laughter creates overtones that communicate throughout other dimensions and is a great medium for growth; and to help others laugh is a very high purpose, you may be sure.

Another practical demonstration — to help you see how easy it is to communicate to other dimensions or to become aware of them and of what you may have to do in order to "tune in" — is to sit at a piano, holding down the sustaining pedal again and to sing in your most rich and resonant voice, one long note. You will hear a repetition or echo of your own tone and corresponding tones. It is an exciting experiment. It does take a certain kind of concentration — the same kind of concentration and exactness with the mind that you use in altered states. Don't be discouraged if you don't make it on the first few tries. Keep on trying. You may even need to try a different piano. The more resonant and bright the piano's sound is, the better your chances. A piano with a "muddy" or muffled sound will not vibrate as much. At any rate, do not expect the sound of the overtone to be very loud. It varies.

When we go into altered states, we are causing vibrations to occur in other dimensions, paving the way for us or even causing the dimension to move toward us. We use these terms but there is no actual distance involved.

INSPIRATION FROM BOOKS

We will sometimes hold onto the most obscure reference and use it as a reminder or catalyst for our growth in enlightenment. This happens when we are ready and not before. Books such as this one lie on a shelf until someone says, "All right. I think I will start looking past my nose now. I think it is about time to play out the ultimate, most exciting game and adventure. I have been saving it up for the last because it is so sweet, so exciting, so fulfilling, so healing, so wonderful, so loving, so self-loving. I think I have paid my dues, and how wonderful now to have this game to go on to. What a relief from the boredom of experiences that have become tiresome and have lost their fun and excitement for me. Okay, I deserve it now. Let's see... page one..."

SHOCK OR STRESS

Physical universe trance states on the "lower" spectrum can be induced by injury, shock, duress, long periods of unrelieved stress, too great a water depth or too long at great depths. (Even the act of putting the head under water induces a slight change in trance state.) There are many ways in which one can move into lower *physical universe trance states*. Even drugs.

DRUGS

Since drugs are unpredictable, the experience is somewhat of a grab bag. One hopes for rapture and spiritual flights into the *Real Realities*, but rarely does that occur. Experiencing the physical universe in a distorted way is not viewing *Real Reality*. It is merely viewing distortion. Now, when it does occur, as a general rule, the *being* has a very difficult time getting it back and may live for years with hope of reexperiencing the freedom of being able to understand and view parts of *Real Reality*.

When we develop the ability to go into altered states for the purpose of enlightenment, we never have to depend upon a substance or even another person to ensure that the experience occurs. We can move into altered states without losing control of the event. When we view dimensions removed from this one, our awareness expands with each visit. We become even more able to perceive. We become ever more able to understand and even participate in the activity. Those under drugs must only accept that which happens. There is no real control and one is left with greater, but limited, understanding. It is similar to either playing in a game or watching it. With drugs, we can only be spectators, not participants. There is also the damage to body tissue with the use of drugs and a great possibility of damage to the connection between the body and the psyche, creating hallucination rather than *Real Reality*.

One way to really mark the difference between a naturally created altered state and one from drugs or other substances is the form the memory takes. States induced by drugs and other substances are recalled in a series of **still** pictures or perceptions whereas natural states are literally reexperienced in present time and are perceived as **moving** thought or pictures.

Trance Levels and Growing Reality

Let it be understood that we in no way wish to denigrate or invalidate any experience which may have occurred with the use of drugs. We would only ask how many times the wish to reexperience the event, to get back the feeling of freedom, to recapture the reality, has crossed the mind?

When we learn to connect with *All There Is* through our own abilities of consciousness, we don't have to **wish** to return. It is available to us at any time. Practice and the decision are all we need. Our reality grows each time we reach into other universe realities. Our abilities to accept that which is different — that which is strange to this physical world — grow stronger.

As we become more aware of *Real Reality*, we begin to view all of life so much more as a game and as a vehicle for learning and experience — and yes, even **fun**. The rewards of awareness are great.

The Sleep State

The "altered state" that is our most usual is the **state of sleep**. We go into a state every time we close our eyes and withdraw from the analytical state of being awake.

In this state of sleep we surrender ourselves to our inner thoughts, inner voice and inner knowing. It is a refreshing relief from the *physical universe trance state*.

Studies have been made in which people were deprived of their dream states within the sleep period. They became very nervous, agitated and incapable of making sound decisions. The reason was that a continuous involvement with the *physical universe trance state* is injurious to the psyche. It is too concentrated a state to experience without the relief that the sleep state affords. Sleep is food for the spirit.

Now the dreaming within the sleep state is a semiphysical universe translation of all we experience when we are free of the *physical universe trance state*. Vivid dreams occur as an attempt on our parts to bring back into this universe concepts grasped during our sleep. These dreams can usually be deciphered after awakening and some of the message at least can be recaptured. It is a good idea to try to awaken with the dream state having completed itself.

There are times, when no matter how careful we are, we find

ourselves awakening from sleep and feeling out of sorts. This is because certain dreams/experiences have not come to a final conclusion. It is not always convenient to go back to sleep, so the conclusion may either work itself out during quiet periods of the day, during a short nap or even the next night. If you have ever experienced a sudden recall or even half-recall of last night's dream as you crawl into bed, that is a sure sign that it wasn't quite finished and that you are preparing to go back and complete the cycle.

A Change in State Changes Our Viewpoint of Action

It is true, also, that at times we move through states that feel like thick clouds of negativity in which we see all the suffering and negative aspects and evidences of this world. We may become supersensitive to our environment and find it grossly lacking and even quite dangerous. This reaction comes about when we have suffered a lot ourselves and we keenly recognize it in others and in the society's make-up. This is a period to come **through** and **out** the other side. It is not one in which to remain. It may even come as a result of looking closely for the first time at the realities that others are projecting.

There is also the reality that we awaken to: the reality of compassion for societal "victims" and anger at societal inequities. This consciousness brings with it a deep desire to change conditions within the society. This is a special kind of awareness and, when focused well, can create more awareness in others in such a way as to bring about changes in these inequities.

The supersensitivity mentioned above actually stands in the way of our power to change conditions. That is why we need to come out of the feeling of negativity regarding our societal problems. What occurs during the focusing of our compassionate energies is a more pragmatic view of conditions with great energies toward creating changes: to come up into the dimension just above that of empathy and sympathy into a strong purpose and drive.

Sympathy is draining and soon becomes apathy, so we come up into the dimension of energy just above it into action and purpose.

When we look at the differences in these two viewpoints — that of experiencing negativity, feeling sympathy and empathy, and then the energy of purpose with positive drive — we have an excellent example of the changes in dimension. These two viewpoints lie close but in different dimensions of awareness. Get the idea? That's why no viewpoint is wrong. Just different. When one is operating on a trance level close to the level of another *being*, it is easier to bring that other *being* up a notch, than to try to bring up one who is operating many levels away. This is why many drives for donations fail because once the *being* comes up to being able to sympathize, nothing is done about what is seen until there is felt a focused drive toward the reality of being able to change conditions. One peeks into that new level and says, "By golly, we **can** do something about this." Sympathy flies out the window and action with purpose flies in.

Now, take a look at the *being* who is further away from sympathy or action of purpose — someone who started from nothing and built an empire. "I did it myself, so can they, and they're not going to get my help." This one is unmoved and feels no sympathy and no empathy because all drives are focused toward self-survival. There is no concern for the survival of others.

Then there are others who are so frightened of experiencing deep deprivation that they are not about to allow themselves to feel anything for the plight of others.

The consciousness of the plight of others, especially in a societal sense brings one much closer to the realization of *Oneness* — that feeling of true kinship with others.

Sharing Trance Levels and Recognizing Projections

We do tend to become more attuned to other realities as we become more aware of everything around us. It is hard, sometimes, to separate projections which belong to us and those which belong to others. If we understand that it could be another's projections, then it is easier to begin to differentiate between ours and theirs. It is inviting, however, to lay all frightening or enigmatic projections on to others, refusing to confront our own images.

You may have experienced riding through another city or several cities and towns on a trip. There is a definite difference in the "feeling" between one town or one city and another. There are even different "flows" evident between one part of town and another. It is more striking if the city is unfamiliar and our own projections and memories are not involved. It makes for a good experiment. Whole areas can share similar trance levels.

There are even different attitudes apparent on different days of the week. The day before a holiday is filled with psychic excitement and a feeling of impending joy: the excitement of being off work and free to be on your own with friends and family. The projections are contagious. We get caught up in them and by doing so, we are interacting with our community in a very productive and creative way, sharing trance levels.

There are so many times and ways we share trance levels. Sporting games, theater, concerts, common disasters all open the way for sharing realities — therefore trance levels.

An added bonus is the fact that with greater understanding and greater reality comes greater ability to understand and enjoy this plane. These are not preachings. Merely statements of fact. Remember, to expect the physical universe to validate our greater awareness or to produce it for us is to ultimately go deeper into *physical universe trance states* rather than up and out. It is our own inner knowing which will validate our abilities, not the physical universe.

Understand, each of us creates our own states of consciousness. We may share states, but they are still our own individual creations, just as all our experiences are — our emotions, understandings, realizations, pain — all are of our own making.

How We Can Help Others

How can we use this knowledge to help bring our friends into states in which they can open up to enlightenment? We can be sources of inspiration, not harassment. We can grant rightness to the games they want to play without entering into those games ourselves. We can continue to grow in enlightenment, acting as mirrors of their true selves.

All of this is going to be easier as we enter this age of enlightenment because *beings* will become ever more ready to grow and learn and remember. There are those who are ready and are waiting for our books, lectures, inspirations, and are waiting to see that we care and that growth and change are indeed possible. They need to know that we are all on the same road no matter what vehicle we use for getting ahead. The message is the same. The end product is the same. All vehicles are necessary because some prefer one frame of reference to another or one viewpoint from another.

Conscious Changes in States

We can will ourselves into an altered state and have done this so many, many times — even daily. We do it just before an interview, just before opening the door to guests, after answering the phone and hearing who is on the line. The person or persons to be faced have a lot to do with the state in which we choose to face them.

"Oh, Alice hates it when I'm sad. Better put on a happy mood for her." "My boss is at the door. Better to assume a worried countenance over this inadequate budget." "I feel like screaming but my five-year-old cries easily, so warm up, mother." "There are so many people on the bus and I'm sure they are all looking at my torn coat, so I'd better be quiet and try to melt into the seat." Get the idea? These are all **conscious** changes in states of mind. We send ourselves into states all the time. We **decide** and **choose** the state from moment to moment. Sometimes we have to really stretch it with great effort in order to keep on a good face or avoid causing a scene, or even to accept a new idea which we "know" is true but would rather not admit it.

The Mind

Now, let's take another viewpoint of these states. What is involved here: the mind or the spirit? Since the spirit does not change but is merely a part of the experience, then it would stand to reason that the mind is the one that changes. With the use of the mind — which is not the brain or even a part of the body, but rather that instrument we devised to stand between the physical universe and the spirit — we see that the mind is a sort of puppet that we manipulate, to help us play games here. We feed it data, store data in it, use it to create habits for us and use it for thinking. Without it we would not be involved. We would not engage in thinking. We consider we have "lost" it when we are no longer able to relate to this universe the same as or similarly to those around us. If we go off too far, our friends begin to worry that we are "losing" our minds.

The true state of the spirit is that of perfection. Perfection before we enter this trance state and perfection when we leave it.

As we begin to lift out of our lower *physical universe trance states*, we are actually coming **out** of our trance by degrees. What we consider altered states are actually closer to our *Real Reality* state of being. Emotions, as we experience them on this plane, are products of this plane.

Emotions and Trance States

We might say that each emotional state resides in a level of the *physical universe trance states* and that emotions are created as an exercise by the mind. So there are levels within levels. All emotions are holographic by nature with all other emotions existing within each one. Even these levels or dimensions within the physical universe dimension contain parts of each other, depending upon the individual. We even have the capacity to **create** a dimension in which to experience an event or situation or even space or time. There is no certainty that we all share in every dimension so created.

Now since all emotions exist within each level — to some degree — we can see how it is that one can be grieving peacefully with great relief at having a trying time pass into history. One can cry in ecstasy, one can feel a peaceful sadness or have angry tears or happy tears or sob deep sobs while experiencing great fear. One can feel happy while experiencing a loss, or experience deep satisfaction at being able to express violent anger. "Mixed feelings" are everyday occurrences.

Realities and Trance States

There are bands upon bands or levels of the *physical universe trance states* and on each of these, realities are different. In order to change a reality it is necessary to come out of one band or level of consciousness and into another. Because we think of "good" as being higher than "bad," we refer to lower and higher levels of consciousness. Now, let's choose a lower level of consciousness — that level that carries with it certainty of evil, evil purposes, "dark side" of nature, the reality of Hell, definitely monsters, certainty of attacks from outer space, "kill him before he kills me," suspicions of all persons different from self (also deep fear of them), and on and on in the same vein.

Now, a look at a level slightly above would show us the same, only a little lighter and less certain. A level above would show us even less certainty but a definite "feeling" about such things, and a light occurrence could tip them on down to lower levels. At such levels the idea of *spirit guides*, or even that people are spirits and not bodies, only brings on derisive laughter.

On each level of *physical universe trance state* we find a complete set of realities endemic to that level or state. It is as though we walk through rooms that contain not only furniture but ideas, certainties, realities, pictures, experiences as well as other *beings* who share many of those same realities. We tend to gravitate to those who share our states — our realities.

You may say, "But George believes in Hell but doesn't believe in attacks from outer space. How can he be on that level?" These states are not physical bands stacked one upon the other, neatly and all packaged up. They are **states of mind — of consciousness**. The less conscious we are, the further we are from *Real Reality*. The less conscious we are, the more distorted our view of our world. There are levels within levels. Each of us creates our own realities. They may be similar, and various facets of them may be agreed-upon, but our levels of awareness are our own. We waft in and out of "bands" which contain the basic pieces of existence that are real within that "band," and the details of our own realities fill in the blank spots. There are infinite ways of putting realities together to form beliefs. These are our most intimate creations and we create them a few at a time, taking great care with their formations.

It is not unusual to experience more than one trance state at a time. In fact, the only way we can experience states outside the *physical universe trance states* is by keeping a toehold on this plane while doing so. When we evolve to the point that we no longer find this universe interesting — not because it is giving us anguish but because we really see through its magic and understand it so well that it has lost its fascination — then we are ready to leave it and probably will. There is little danger of that occurring without our knowing it, planning for it and realizing it, however. We hardly need worry about reading a book and finding ourselves dead on the floor. There is a lot of game left for all of us and this last phase is already beginning to be our most exciting involvement yet.

CHAPTER NINE

GHOSTS, POLTERGEISTS, DEMONS, MONSTERS AND OTHER SPIRITS

Ghosts and goblins and things that go bump in the night! All children grow up learning to fear the world from which they came. It is the same phenomenon that raises the hair on the neck when someone believed to be dead begins to move or open the eyes. The body that was so dear a moment before is now looked upon with fear.

To the degree we have forgotten that we too are *spirits*, we can be afraid of bodiless entities. Once we realize we **are** a part of **everything** that is and **everyone** that is, the fear vanishes. There is nothing whatever to fear on any plane or dimension.

Physical manifestations of bodies very unlike our own are formed in the imagination and projected in various stages of physical reality — ranging from pictures in the mind to wispy cloud-like forms, to shadowy or glowing representations, of bodily formations all the way to solid form, such as our own bodies represent. Indeed, our bodies are projections as well, having source outside this physical universe — much as you, as a *spirit*, actually reside outside this physical universe for the most part.

We **will** see demons and monsters if we expect to. In other words, our expectations, our imaginations, are the "creators." That is the **way** we create our worlds — so to that extent such entities do exist.

Once these entities take birth and form from our imaginative thought, they do exist and as such must be dealt with in one way or another. The best tools for dealing with them is love and laughter.

If we love our creations, they will fade away. If we create them, then become fearful, angry or violent, they will only grow and last. We may create things we do not want to lose even if we love them. They will last as long as we keep them "real" in our minds. Our monsters will also fade away if we finally take all attention off them for a period of time and do not continue to reinforce them with our thoughts and fears.

Our projections live on that which created them. If fear creates a monster, then it takes fearful attention to hold on to it. If it is created with love, then loving attention will perpetuate it. Apathy and inattention will cause it to fade — finally into nonexistence.

Once in a while we may perceive another's projections. We can laugh and admire them and they will disappear for us.

Whatever we create and behold in our imaginations is true or it wouldn't have occurred to us. We can trust our imaginations and know that whatever occurs to us is true on some level, plane or time, lasting for millions of years to only a flash of a moment.

Our thoughts create waves of matter and near-matter which are used on other planes as raw materials for forming realities. We use the raw materials that project themselves into this plane in much the same way.

If particles of matter were reduced down to the lowest common denominator, we would find units of spirituality with sentience and drives, purposes and awarenesses of their own. They perhaps do not have a conscious awareness of us as we view ourselves, but consciousness nonetheless — not **below** or **above** our own — but different, with different goals and experiences sought after.

What Is a Ghost?

A ghost, for purposes of common, agreed-upon definition, is a *spirit* or *being* who once occupied a physical body and who has the ability to, in some way, make itself known to those still occupying bodies. Ghosts have not left the *physical universe trance states*.

The ability to project an outline or shadow or wispy or even more solid representation of a past incarnation is done by a highly concentrated level of intention. Famous ghosts in England, for instance, have practiced until their performances are near-perfect. These are *beings* who are no longer caught in between dimensions but are literally residing on levels similar to those used while in a body. They are "stuck" in a sense, in an old event — either of death or the death of someone close to them. They have gradually begun to relate to the present time and the past simultaneously. They do not realize that there is more to life and they seem to enjoy life as it is for them.

Many times ghosts are held in a spot or an area in which they met with a violent or otherwise intense end. Not all ghosts can be seen, however, but may be "sensed" or "felt" or almost glimpsed out of the corner of the eye. Some may be heard. They may have gained the ability to produce sound, if not sight, impressions such as knocking, rattling, wind sounds or even vocal sounds.

Fearing a ghost makes as much sense as fearing a puff of smoke from a pipe.

For the most part, ghosts are *beings* who continue to relive an incident of great emotional impact. They seem to be unable to realize they are no longer residing in a body. Their relationships to those within bodies are even more wispy than ours with them. In fact, many ghosts never see us at all. They are existing more or less in the time frame of their time of death. Their own fear has continued to solidify the event in which they have become encysted. So when we perceive a ghost, we are literally perceiving a **past** event.

Entire battles have been fought, over and over again, and from time to time people in the present have been able to watch the ghostly battle taking place. If only **one** *spirit* is caught up in the vortex of a repetitive experience, then we see only **one** ghost, but if more than one is so caught up, then we perceive them as well.

Some ghosts have ended their trail of terror but due to the effect they can create, have lingered on to enjoy the game of being ghosts. These are usually happy individuals, perhaps a little mischievous, and they enjoy the role they play. They are no longer existing in the past but can relate to the present and even carry on "conversations" of one kind or another.

Other ghosts may finally begin to perceive the present and, because they are motivated by fear, may cause havoc in a house for the people who live there. They may stomp through rooms, hoping the inhabitants will leave. Their only "power" lies in the fear the inhabitants exhibit.

These ghosts are in great trouble and need love, compassion and understanding to help them break free. They are usually projecting pictures of the event, who they are and circumstances surrounding the event itself. A good medium can perceive these pictures, communicate with the ghost, show understanding and the ghost will usually have a realization and leave of its own accord.

The practice of damning, cursing or sending the *spirit* into a black hole forever or even shooting it into the void are all results of fear and misunderstanding on the part of the medium.

Imagine finding oneself in a similar position and one can quickly see that fear and anger will not help a *spirit* in trouble.

Ghosts are no different from anyone else. They are *beings* no more strange than you are. Life on this plane invites the idea of separation and individuation. The key to the opening of the door of knowledge, understanding and awareness is the realization of "belonging" to *All There Is*. With that realization comes the greatest peace and happiness that exist.

There are ghosts who stay in a place because they like it. They eventually become bored and they leave to fulfill the "end of life" ritual (for want of a better word).

There are *beings* stuck under rocks and underwater — wherever they met a violent end. There are *beings* stuck in caves, near graves or in them. There are others who are "guarding" or "defending" areas (buildings, rooms, bits of real estate, caves); anywhere a *being* **could** get stuck, one or more can usually be found. If they are stuck in time as well as space, they may not be able to come loose easily or even be able to perceive anyone in our present time frame. They may even be "asleep," but some mediums can nudge them awake and eventually help them free themselves from an unproductive situation.

Ghosts usually appear or are perceived at the same age as death occurred. There are child ghosts and old-age ghosts.

There are animal ghosts as well. Cats can be seen walking through a house in which they lived. Dogs can be seen running in neighborhoods in which they ran while alive in the body. Sometimes an animal can be "seen" guarding the grave of a beloved friend.

"Live" Ghosts

There are *beings* in bodies who are so intent upon being in a place that they unknowingly project themselves into the place; and if there are those around who can perceive of such things, they can be seen as ghosts. The key is the intensity, not effort, that is employed in the desire and the degree of reality that is assumed.

There are many stories of family members who live thousands of miles away, yet are seen in wispy form in the presence of parents, children, brother or sisters. Most times they are unaware that there is a projection at all.

This is the same process that is used by our *guides* when we "see" them. The intensity of desire and the intention to be seen are employed. The reason we can see a ghost at all is that the belief that the *being* is still there in the place where the death or other such traumatic event took place is so strong that a projection naturally occurs.

If you were to have an intense desire to be walking on a particular beach, then you would actually walk upon that beach without your body. If the intention were great enough, a projection of your body would appear on that beach and anyone around who was aware enough would actually see it.

Monsters

Demons, monsters and other scary entities are merely projections by self or others. Most often they are products of our own fears and uncertainties. They go away quickly with laughter and humor at the ludicrousness of the truth of their existence. They have no power of their own, no reality of their own, no *beingness* of their own, yet they are to be dealt with in some manner, even if it is to acknowledge them, knowing they will eventually disappear. Laughter and intention toward their disappearance will do the trick, as we said before. Fears of the mind can be dealt with in the same way — even when there are no projections. We have all experienced throwing off old fears. Fearful resistance never works. It only intensifies the reality.

Sometimes a ghost will be able to throw out a projection. When it meets with humor and love, the *being* usually becomes unable to continue the intensity because it takes an enormous amount of energy to keep it alive. Without your fear-energy, they usually even lose interest. Some projections finally fade if no one perceives them and they slip into other dimensions to be used as raw materials for other "creations."

There was a time in our "distant past" when we all played around with such projections, making them ever more solid. We would then all collapse with laughter and they would begin to disappear. The more we laughed, the harder it was to keep them in place. Most of us have forgotten this and when we see them now we become afraid.

Those who love to see horror films are experiencing some of the old pattern of: create, be fearful of, laugh at and destroy. Those who can truly confront violence, "evil," demonic apparitions on film, and can find them entertaining and funny are those who may probably never have to confront them in actual physical existence, or they have already done so in the past. There are those of course who do not actually confront such things but create them solidly within the mind, becoming ever more fearful. These are the ones who will have to experience violence and terror on actual physical terms — that is, unless they go through other changes in the meantime which render them unafraid. Many such *beings* are experiencing physical form for the first time or are relatively new to this plane. There is **no** experience that a *being* **has** to have. Nothing is set up for us in that way.

Poltergeists

A poltergeist is a *being* who is having a tantrum. He is in trouble and the last thing on his mind is the thought of hurting anyone. He, more than likely, doesn't even know you exist and if he does, he only wants your help. The ideas that a poltergeist is an entity that is displaying mischievousness or is intent upon frightening others or is just hinting at the greater danger that he could cause are all false.

There are those who would swear to the powers they have observed by entities who move furniture around, break windows, slam doors and try to attack people. There are energy sources that are available on this dimensional physical plane that are strong enough to accomplish such feats. A *being* who is caught in a lower, more solid *physical universe trance state* can, with the added power of fear engendered in people, create impressive feats of "magic." It is rare, but it can happen. Without the fear energies donated by frightened people, however, the effects are far less impressive and are no more than those of any ordinary poltergeist. And just as in the case of the young girl in puberty who shoots energies around, not realizing they are her energies, the poltergeist may not even know the effects that are being created are his.

As in any tantrum, be it from a child, adult or bodiless entity, the effect wished for is recognition of existence. Once a *being* is recognized and acknowledged as a *being* who **deserves** respect, love, understanding and recognition, the tantrum stops and healing can occur. Anyone engaged in a tantrum is doing so only in order to gain these recognitions. If you are around such a *being*, understand this and quietly acknowledge him. Indicate that for the space of time it takes him to calm himself down he will be ignored so as not to embarrass him further: the tantrums will finally cease. If we become angry, however, or afraid, such an acknowledgment becomes impossible because it is very hard to recognize or acknowledge anyone with respect, love and understanding when we are so emotional. Our anger and fear serve as gasoline to the fire of the hysteria, just as our fear of the entity feeds the power of his abilities to create physical effects.

The nature of the energies called upon are such that they cause hair to stand on end, which leads to adrenaline shooting through the body, preparing it for flight or fight. This, then, tends to awaken old fears, bringing them to the fore and before we know it, we have dipped down into a lower *physical universe trance state* and entered into full-fledged terror; and as we add our own projections and pictures of fears, unknown and known, we find ourselves engaged in the poltergeist's tantrum. This is how, with the aid of our power, great effects are possible. This is how we fan the fires of that energy.

Beings Caught between Levels of Consciousness

What we have here is a *being* "caught between" layers or levels of the *physical universe trance states.* He is so caught because of the intensity of his *death experience.* He may or may not need to tell you what it was. Remember, even if you cannot "hear" him, you can perceive his presence through the energies you experience. Do not worry if you are not hearing the story of his death. It is really unimportant. The important thing is that he can hear **you.**

We **can** feel and perceive the effects of these energies without going further into the scenario. We **can** withstand the goose bumps and hair-raising sensations. We **can** stand firm and state aloud or telepathically that we realize the *being* deserves recognition, respect, love and understanding and that we are there to grant these to the entity. We can tell the entity that he is "caught between" levels of consciousness and needs our help. At this point we have the being's total attention and the effects will subside somewhat.

Tell the *being* that you know he has had a very hard time and needs to forgive those who appear to have caused his troubles. After he has done so, indicate further that he can perhaps forgive himself (we don't need to specify for what) and that God has forgiven him and that we have forgiven him as well. He will calm down further.

If you cannot perceive his answers, just monitor your own

physical sensations. As you begin to calm down, you can be sure he is also. Proceed with certainty that what you are doing is working. Do not back out. You are the only one at that point that can be of aid to the entity. He knows that too, and wants your help. If you do not feel certainty, then pretend you do and proceed. Remember, do not go too slowly. They move fast when they begin to move.

There may be more than one *being* in the same area and you may have to do the process more than once. Once you read this data and understand it, you will be able to help many *beings* who are "caught between".

Energy Screen

Sometimes, when one *being* frees himself, others will be observing and will free themselves at the same time. You may perceive this. Many times you may think there are more *beings* there, but what you are perceiving may be clouds of disturbed mental energies. Usually black. Some can see it but most of us can feel it. In that case, all you have to do is create in your mind a large, flat screen made of energy.

Create the screen large enough to cover the size of the house, building or area of ground. Imagine the screen being created at least ten feet below the surface. Now bring it up slowly through the floor or earth, carrying with it all disturbed mental energies. Bring it up slowly through the roof to go about two hundred and fifty feet above. Now imagine that the energy dissipates and melts away at that height. If, after the first sweep of the screen, you still perceive the energy, do it a second or third time and by then it should have left. This is a very good process for any room in which there have been troubled persons, arguments or deep upsets. It can be done with no one ever knowing or realizing it has been done.

There are many abilities we possess and all we need is to be reminded of them.

Not in Spirit World

An important thing to realize about these *beings* "caught between" is that they are not in what we know of as the *spirit world*. They are still a part of the physical world. This is why their *guides* have not been able to help them. They may have been stuck for a week or thousands of years. You have the opportunity to act as *spirit guide* in these situations. Once you do, you will have much greater reality on your own *spirit guides* and their motives.

There are people we know who are living life, working at jobs, are lucid and coherent, who cannot in any way relate to the *spirit world*. How could we possibly expect a *being* to relate to the *spirit world* who is much "lower" in the *physical universe trance states*, who has lost his body in a violent or intense death, has been going around in circles ever since, reliving that life over and over again or has been having tantrums because he is confused and doesn't know where he is? He may also be experiencing Hell or whatever he thought he would experience after death. This is why we bring them "back into the physical universe."

Reorientation

We might even suggest that they get their bearings, so to speak — become reoriented to this plane before they communicate with their *spirit guides* who will help them in their next step.

We may suggest that they fly over the beautiful cities of New York, London and Paris, enjoy great blue bodies of water, rivers, countryside and share the experiences with their *spirit guides* who wish to aid in their healing.

In this way we have not only helped them back into the upper levels of the *physical universe trance state* but have reacquainted them with the reality of the *spirit world*.

It is wise to mention their *spirit guides* so they will automatically begin to relate to them. Otherwise they may just wander for great long periods of time. If, in the excitement of the process, you forget to mention the *spirit guides*, they will eventually find them on their own.

Some of these *beings* are still so traumatized, even after freeing themselves, that they find it hard to move out of our spaces. We can invite them to hang around for a few hours or even days until they have reoriented themselves to this plane. The very idea of flying about, looking at anything, is a horrifying prospect. In these cases we speak gently and tell them that as soon as they perceive two *spirit friends*, they will begin to remember *Real Reality* and no longer feel afraid. The *guides* will appear and more than likely the *being* will go with them, feeling all safe and happy.

The less we resist their staying around us, the less likely they are to stay. You will find they will soon wish to be on their own.

Your Responsibility

Never, never, never feel guilty for what you might judge to be an imperfect process. What is important is that all a *being* really needs to free himself is to know he **can**, and if you have trouble in completing the process or in delivering it, never fear. The *being* has been recognized and knows he can free himself. If you only repeated those two things — "I recognize you, and I want you to know that you are caught in between levels of consciousness and you can free yourself" — then you have done a beautiful service. The only thing not to do is to ignore a *being* in trouble or be angry or afraid with him. He is fear personified and your fear just feeds his fear, making it stronger between you.

You may have to console him a bit. Tell him that you know how hard this ordeal has been, but that now it is over and he is free. Hold out your hand and ask him to take it. Tell him that you will pull him out and back into the physical universe where he wants to be. He will do it if you are patient. If he holds back, speak louder and say, "I'm pulling you out **now**!" With your strength and certainty he will follow. If you are weak and uncertain, he may not. You will perceive some relief within yourself and that will be an echoing signal that he has freed himself. As you pull him back, do it slowly with great strength in your muscles. He will respond to that strength.

No Possession

There is absolutely **no danger** in your being possessed during this process. The level of cause of these *beings* is extremely low and that is why they haven't realized they are free. They literally **cannot** possess you. Their feelings, emotions, pains and uncertainties certainly can impinge upon you and that is why you must remain calm, certain and strong. They are drawn in by **your** emotions as well.

There is nothing to fear on being "possessed" by **any** entity. When people feel pressures or feel that a *being* is possessing them, they have only to realize that the entity is trying its best to communicate and that we are merely "tuning in" to the pain or anguish the entity is experiencing. We may experience empathetic pains in parts of the body which correspond to the pains experienced by the entity.

These entities cannot really hurt or kill us. They cannot "make" us do things we wouldn't ordinarily do. We **may** tune in to moods or emotions that are common to our own but that is as far as the influence can go. We may realize that the emotion we are feeling is not appropriate to the present situation and that may be a clue to the presence of an entity.

If, however, we allow fear to take over, we can dip into the lower corresponding state and share in the experience of the entity. When we allow that to happen, we render ourselves incapable of helping the entity as well as causing ourselves a few uncomfortable days. It will wear off for us, but the entity will **still** be suffering as usual.

Be assured that any and all emotions you experience are always **yours**. Even if you are tuned into emotions of entities or others, what you "feel" is yours.

NO ONE CAN CREATE AN EMOTION IN YOU.
YOU CREATE YOUR OWN.

Unstable Beings and Those Caught Between

There are those who have given all or most of their power to chance and have fallen between the cracks of our societies. We sometimes call them insane, retarded and many less compassionate names. These *beings* are experiencing lower depths of causation and are not in control of their lives in the same way the rest of us are. They are experiencing a certain lack of responsibility and a definite lack of power as *beings*.

When these unstable *beings* "tune in" to *beings* "caught between," the bonding is much more complete than with a *being* who is merely depressed. This explains why we see unstable beings walking the streets talking to themselves. Those "caught between" are communicating their feelings and scenarios, rambling on and on and those unstable beings are actually *channeling* in a haphazard sort of way. It is almost as if a **group** is walking around near one body, and this is the closest to "possession" we are likely to come. There is a sort of sharing of body, in a sense. The person who owns the body is "caught between" himself.

Now, if we were to free the *beings* who are tuned in to the unstable person, that person would still need some help in regaining enough power to improve his existence. Otherwise, he will "tune in" to other entities.

Many times, however, with the release of the entities, the *being* is free to realize his condition and come up enough to want to create changes in his life. So you never know when you telepathically help a *being* you see on the street just how much influence you have wielded. One thing is for sure — you have helped free *beings* who otherwise would not have been freed.

You Are the Pivot

The way you know for certain that a *being* has responded to you is that the character of **your** feelings will slightly change. (Even if you are working on someone else — remember, we are **one**). It may be subtle, but don't wait for more confirmation. Just go on with the process.

You are the pivot around which this event takes place. You are the one in charge. You are the one with the most awareness in this instance. Your soft, firm commands — "Take my hand and I will pull you out" and "I know you exist and I feel great respect for you and for what you have gone through. I love you and understand your problems" — are what will set the stage for his release. Get the idea? That is what a *being* wants to hear and that recognition is all he needs, really, to free himself. But he may also be afraid of the newness of the experience and it is up to you to console and inspire him to be free.

Do not be surprised if you get halfway through your process of helping him free himself (for he is the only one who can) and you find yourself standing alone, with no sensations left. Many times they are so thrilled to be free that they leave instantly.

Wanting to Stop

If, during the process, you hear yourself saying "I can't go through with this" or "This is all too frightening and I'm not going on with it," or any such thing, you are surely receiving telepathic communication from the entity. **He** is the one who wants to stop. **He** is the one who is afraid. You can depend upon this data 100%. All you have to do is realize that those are his thoughts and realize that for him they are even more real than they **seem** to be for you.

When the entity has had the opportunity to free himself, the pains and anguish will disappear for you as well. The only reason this phenomenon can occur is because of the natural tie that binds all *beingness* together. The oneness and the fact of being a part of all life everywhere is what makes such help possible.

If you feel this terrible urge to stop, just console him and give him a pep talk, telling him he **can** make it. It will also benefit you.

Remember, the important person here is the *being* ''caught between.'' Those in bodies are in fine shape in comparison, so our sympathies are with the *being* who feels he cannot free himself.

Our Attitudes Toward ''Lost Souls'' Are Important

It is a rare and beautiful thing to be able to help our friends who are in trouble. It is also our duty to help when we can because our *guides* cannot penetrate the lower levels of consciousness. It is up to us to bring these entities up without force, but with recognition, love, respect and understanding. A show of certain loving strength is sometimes enough to have the *being* realize himself and go free. Force, anger, fright or revulsion can cause a *being* to recede, burying himself deeper into his plight and prolonging his ''entrapment.''

In the past and on a small scale now in the present, there have been those who have treated such ''lost souls'' in ways that were less godly. Shooting them off to other spheres (lower depths of *physical universe trance states*), sending them to ''Hell'' or through black holes to be ''lost forever.'' All these suggestions take root in the lower trance states in which they obey the command. How much better to give them the command to go free.

A *being* caught in the lower levels of consciousness and who has lost his body may think **any** body is his body. That is how we are sometimes able to communicate with them. They **can** relate to bodies, because they think *beings* **are** bodies. Our bodies act much as ''windows'' and doors through which such lost entities can come through and back into the upper levels of the *physical universe trance state*. Until he does, he is not at all a candidate for higher awareness. It helps to picture him in your mind as a well and happy *being*, meeting his *guides* and going on to new life. It is only through freedom from their own unawareness which we are capable of showing them that they can begin to awaken.

If any of this frightens you, just realize that you are merely frightened of your own perceptions and that **nothing** can happen to you that you are not able to endure and handle successfully. The more practice you have, the easier it becomes.

It is not suggested that we try to instill "beliefs" into the entities we assist. Only that they can free themselves, that they are loved, respected, recognized and understood and that they may wish to reorient themselves to the physical world. To do anything else is to try to interfere with their own determination and may even serve to prolong their confusion.

Whenever you feel an emotion or are feeling out of sorts, it is not necessarily because of another *being* who is trying to communicate. These occurrences are rare and **all** of your emotions are your own. Even when a *being* is near you with an uncomfortable emotion, what you feel is still your own. You have merely "tuned in" to that vibration in an empathetic way. It will almost always, however, result in a magnification of your own feelings, causing an increase in intensity of the emotional experience. Once the *being* is released, the magnification is reduced and you are left with only your own feelings and emotions. They, then, can be dealt with more easily.

Distorted Perceptions

Now, if a *being* is "caught between" two of these lower states, he is sharing, in a distorted view, realities on both levels between which he is caught. Such distortion is frightening and the entity is experiencing not only that but is going in circles reexperiencing his death over and over again. In such levels, death is the absolute worse thing that can happen to a *being* so the fear is intense. He is neither in the physical universe as we know it nor is he in the *spirit world*. He is deep into a lower *physical universe trance state*.

There are those few who are so caught up in an event preceding death that the death itself is less important. For instance, a father who dies in a fire may be more caught up in his child's safety than in his own death. He may spend many years trying to find and save the child as he wanders the gray, distorted world between levels of consciousness.

All Beings "Caught Between" Are Not on the Same Level

A *being* can be caught in a higher level of consciousness and still be reexperiencing a death over and over again. It all depends upon the state of consciousness in which the experience is felt. They can be caught in a childlike innocence and waft back and forth up and down a hall or flight of stairs. They may merely be caught in a perpetual sadness and confusion. These are what we usually refer to as ghosts. If they perceive those who are alive in bodies at all, they are more frightened than we are at perceiving them. They can be handled with the same process. The wispy form will disappear before the *being* has left, however, so the process should be continued as described.

Once in a while we may discover a *being* who is very angry and hard to help. We may even return anger to them, not really wishing to help. It is hard to feel understanding, love, respect and recognition, much less forgiveness in such cases. These are great opportunities for self-growth and enlightenment. To handle with grace one who is not desirous of help and who is angry and is visiting all those vibrations upon you is to lift yourself into a higher state of awareness. He is indeed doing you a service.

Recognizing and Understanding Their Realities and Courage

A *being* may even say he hates God, hates you and hates everyone. He thinks he hates himself and that he deserves to be hated. If we believe what he says and become afraid, judgmental and angry with him, then we render ourselves incapable of helping. We can realize that he is experiencing a lower level of consciousness, of awareness, and he is only aware of what he sees there. Even if he exudes what seems to be evil, complete with threats, he is only projecting what he sees and what he is experiencing.

One has to greatly admire such a *being* for exercising great courage in reaching from such a depth. Think of it. Here is a *being* on the lower rungs of the consciousness ladder, yet has the innate knowledge that there is something better. He communicates in the only way he can but such communication comes through many thick and quite solid levels and that takes great courage.

You can be sure that any such *being* is doing all he can to pull himself up. It wouldn't hurt to display some admiration for him along with the recognition, respect, love and understanding.

We, on the other hand, are aware of a whole different set of realities. We are aware that he sees one thing and we another, but he is not aware of what we see. It is up to us, if we choose to help, to speak from our greater view with certainty and love and understanding — recognizing the *being* and respecting him. Respect along with recognition will enable him to come into a higher state, and as the process advances, he comes ever higher and higher until he can see that your body is not his. He can see that he need not be afraid. He can see that he is really free. Get the idea? Until he lifts himself into that higher band, he literally **cannot see** anything except what is there where **he** is in awareness. **He can only sense it** — just as we **sense** the greater realities above our own comprehension.

We can see only those things which are available to our awarenesses at the level of consciousness in which we reside.

It is the desire of our *spirit guides* to lead us into even higher levels of consciousness much in the same way as we desire to help others. They grant us **recognition, love, respect, understanding** and all other spiritual inspiration that we need to help us. Just as we have no intention to help free a *being* and then proceed to map out a life for him, protecting him from every harm, advising him on every decision he makes — our *guides* and *friends* feel much the same about us, except the relationship does continue.

Helping Other Beings on the Spot

For those who are sensitive, there will arise the opportunity to help one who has just left the body in a violent manner. Perhaps an accident or other such mishap will create a confusion for the *being* and he may be drawn to the first safe place he can find. That place may be where you are. There are occasions in which we can direct a *being* back to his body so he can assess whether or not it is injured too deeply to be of further service to him.

In times of great stressful *death experiences* a *being* may go into an instant confused state. He may not even know he is out of the body. He may have had his accident or other violent experience in a place very far away from where you are. By his pictures you can find out where the body is and tell him. In his confusion he thinks he is lost. Simply direct him to the place where the body is.

We can have him notice physical objects around, speak to him and indicate that he is out of his body and that perhaps he needs to go back to it and help it breathe again. This can all be done in an instant.

Speed Is Important

Due to the speed that is being experienced by the *being*, your communication can be telepathically geared to his speed. Your communication will be stronger the **faster** you send it, so don't wait for confirmation of each bit and piece of your thoughts to him. Go at his speed so he can get back to his body if he wishes. He most certainly will be curious about it and wish to see what has happened. After he has done this, you are finished with your part of his experience. There is no need to stick around to see what happens unless you wish.

When he returns to his body he will most likely pick it up again. If it is indeed badly damaged beyond his wish to repair it, he will then be available for communication with his *guides* and will no longer need you. We do not have to worry about a *being* who is well enough spiritually to return to the scene of the "death" on his own accord. He is not "caught between" dimensions and is not likely to become a "lost soul."

This idea of speed in regard to communicating with *beings* applies to all of them. We can hold them back by being too slow. Telepathy travels much faster than vocal language. Sometimes we can flash a picture to a *being* — a picture showing him free and happy and he will get it instantly.

Many Places Where "Lost Souls" Can Be Found

There are sites where accidents, murders or suicides have occurred. Sometimes, years later, we find the "victim" still there. Even great, large groups can be found at sites of old train wrecks and fires. We can use the same processes with these *beings*, freeing them from the perpetual experience into which they have drawn themselves. There are places on highways where accidents have occurred. Mental pictures of these accidents have led some to think they are being told to have an accident. They are really tuning into a being who is "caught between" and is trying to communicate. Those who see such pictures are perceptually aware and can at that point respond by freeing the *being*. There are battlefields where we have great opportunities for aiding in the freedom of many *beings* still fighting ancient wars. There are places everywhere in which we could possibly find a *being* in distress. A short drive through a cemetery can serve some who think they have to stay in the body until Judgment Day. They are all "caught between" dimensions.

There are *beings* who are "caught between" dimensions who are actually "asleep." Some are drug "victims" or left the body in an unconscious state and never came out of it. Those in coma are asleep in the same way. They are "caught between" as well. They can be brought back to the body-consciousness state. Those who are asleep can be awakened gently and brought on up through higher levels. The strength of our intention along with their willingness is what makes it work.

Vulnerability

If you have ever had an operation and experienced coming out of anesthetics — to that point just prior to knowing where you are and what is happening — then you know exactly how a *being* who is "caught between" dimensions is experiencing life. Add to that, horrifying projections or a perpetual *death experience*. The *being* could possibly have been caught there for centuries. Their experiences range from vivid to totally unreal or an experience of nonexistence.

Suppose a *being* is experiencing a *death experience* over and over again or perhaps even experiencing an excruciating hell that he projected as that which was his due. When he finally begins to awaken somewhat, he is vulnerable to suggestion just as one who is under anesthetic is vulnerable.

If, when coming out of anesthetic you were met with "Oh, here is an evil entity — it is taking over my body! Oh, oh, my God! I must get rid of this demon. I must send it into a black hole, out into space, into a void — anywhere but here. I must not let it take over my body. I can feel pains where he must be!" Get the idea? What if you were met with such turmoil, fear and bad wishes and projections?

We Perceive on Telepathic Level

When we perceive our friends in trouble, we will many times take on their sufferings, emotions and attitudes in order to help alleviate them. We do this on a telepathic level, just beneath our analytical knowing and do not consciously remember it. We take on these problems when we, too, are at a low ebb — depressed, ill, in pain, upset, etc. Then each time we dip back into that state, we experience the same things our friends are experiencing — only in a smaller way.

On the other side of the coin, our friend in trouble perceives your body and projects the idea that it is somehow his own, long-lost body — and the co-creation is then complete. You have reached out toward that *being* while at a low ebb. Your suffering is similar to his and the *being* has reached out to you. A type of spiritual "bonding" occurs. This can go on for a day or for many years — each tapping into the other periodically. Many chronic pains and ills stem from this very phenomenon. Each time we dip into that low ebb pattern, we "tune in" to the other *being* and feel the pain.

Helping Others Increases Our Growth

Now, a great beautiful result of such aid as you can give is that with each being so helped, we arrive closer and closer to our own *beingness*, our own *knowingness*. We come up into higher and higher states in which we find ourselves staying longer and longer. We discover that we hardly ever experience lower states which we have hitherto thought of as our "natural" states. We discover the beauty of the upper reaches of awareness. Our lives become closer to our own desires for ourselves. We feel good about ourselves as never before. These advantages come unbidden as we help others. They do not come through great effort but through awareness and the willingness to love without needing an exchange for that love.

Review of Steps to Freeing Beings

After perceiving there is a *being* "caught between":

1. Stand firm, ignoring your own emotions and sensations.
2. State aloud or telepathically that you recognize the *being* is there

and that he exists. (**Recognition.**)

3 . Speak to the *being* with **respect**. Indicate to him that he is **loved** and **understood**. Your attitude must be real.

4 . Be creative. Each *being* is different. Each *being* has experienced his **own** experience.

    a . You may tell him he is "caught between" dimensions and that you can help him free himself.

    b . You may tell him you know he has had a hard time and that it is all over now. It is time for him to free himself.

    c . He may think you are God. Let him. He may believe that only God can free him. He will know the truth soon enough. He will know that he, too, is God.

    d . Agree with him, sympathize with him. Agree with his victimhood. He will trust you if you prove you are on his side. If he is angry, your sympathy with his anger will dissolve it along with much of his anxiety.

    e . Ask him if he can forgive those responsible for his condition. When he does, even a little bit, ask if he can forgive himself. This usually loosens him up and he may lift out at this point.

    f . Tell him he has been forgiven and it is time for him to go on with new life.

5 . Sometimes a *being* cannot free himself until he has talked about his death. Don't **insist** that he talk about it, but if you have gone through all the steps and he still hasn't freed himself, it is because he still hasn't let go of the emotion in the death or predeath experience. Telling you about it will release the hold it has on him and he can change his viewpoint. Remember, you do not actually have to hear it but the more you practice, the sooner you will.

    Being stuck is a viewpoint. Talk to the *being* until he can change his viewpoint. Once he does, he's free.

6 . Hold out your hand, pull him "out" and trust it to happen.

7 . By monitoring your own emotions and sensations you can tell when changes have occurred with our "being in trouble."

8 . Proceed with certainty and speed. The whole process takes only moments or minutes.

9 . If you have gone through all the steps and still "feel" he is there, use the screen to sweep mass out of the way. That is probably all that is left.

10. The last step is to introduce the *being* to two of his *spirit guides*. Now, whether or not you can perceive them, they will appear

to the *being*. From the moment you contact a *being*, the *spirit family* is aware of it and there is no way they **won't** appear. Trust it. You do not have to see them.

Tell the *being* that when he sees his *friends* (*guides*) he will begin to remember **everything** and will know he is safe. If he refuses or rejects his *guides*, tell him he is welcome to stay near you for a while to become reoriented to his new viewpoint. He may welcome the thought of flying across the planet and enjoying the scenery. This will help him to realize his position and then he will most probably "see" his *guides* and join them. At any rate, your involvement is over as soon as he frees himself. He will not "tune in" to you again now that he is free. His interest will be on his own plight. Any interest in you will probably be that of gratefulness and awe.

11. **Remember**: These steps are only meant as a guide, and your perceptions on the spot are what mark the difference between what "generally" happens and what "actually" happens in your experience.

Recognition, respect, love and understanding — as long as these are present you will be rewarded for your compassion. The words themselves do not have to be spoken as long as the meaning can be felt. The main thing is to do the best you can, no matter how inadequate you may feel.

Short Steps for Those Beings Who Respond Easily

Sometimes, we can talk them through it quickly. When we are more adept, we can just allow ourselves to be "led" to speak to them in a certain way.

For example: "I see you, wonderful being. I see you have experienced great pain and anguish. It is time for you to let go of all that now. It is all over. No more pain, fear or anguish. (Allow for a response) Oh, my darling, I know. I know. You have suffered much. Take my hand. (They will sometimes go at this point. If not, continue.) You can do it. Can you forgive those who put you there? Just a little bit? You have been forgiven, you know. (Allow for response.) Can you forgive yourself? Sure you can. Of course you can. It is all over now. You are free. You have only to take my hand and come on back into the physical universe. That's good. You are doing well. **Now**. You are free. Congratulations! How wonderful! Now, I want you to meet two old *friends* of yours. When you see them, you will begin to remember everything. Happy life to you, wonderful being."

You can use variations of that. Do not try to make it a rote process. Each *being* is different. They will "feel" different. Allow yourself to be "led" to speak to them. Their *guides* will help in this way. Your willingness will be rewarded many times over with help and *channeled* assistance from them.

We May Encounter Spirits from the "Astral" Plane

There are *beings* who reside on levels just barely at the top of the *physical universe trance state*. This level is sometimes referred to as the *astral level*. They can view this plane easily and even travel in it, creating small effects, but are not totally involved in it. Those who project themselves into other planes do so on this level. All emotions experienced at this level are clean and free from the darker consciousness of the lower planes. This is why those on that plane often seem giddy and irresponsible to us. They view us much as we view entities caught in lower levels of awareness. They would love to help more but usually do not succeed because by the time we are sufficiently aware of that plane, our *guides* are ready and waiting. So these happy *beings* just trip around, enjoying what they can as they, too, develop through climbing into "higher" levels of consciousness.

On this *astral level* can be found many *beings* who come for a visit from other planes. Our *guides* usually communicate to us from this plane. It is through this plane that interstellar travel is possible. It is through this plane that objects travel when they are dematerialized in one location and rematerialized in another.

Relatives who visit us after body death do so, through the *astral plane*. There are *beings* who love to congregate around parks and pleasant places. They spend a lot of "time" at such places, just enjoying the scenery and watching the people as they pass. This is the level at which certain "ghosts" appear who are not caught in lower levels of trance state. They sometimes wish to act as *spirit guides* and at times have succeeded. They may, for instance, shake a bed, trying to awaken a sleeper who is in danger. There are many stories of such encounters between friendly ghosts and those on our plane.

There are as many *beings* and types of *beings* as we can imagine. We have great and wonderful potentials for creating any kind of *beingness* we wish. We are all chameleons, actors and clowns. We assume many characters even within the scope of one day. We act many, many parts within the scope of a lifetime. The farther we travel beyond the confines of this physical plane, the more varied and exciting our characters become. The farther we go above this plane, the greater becomes the potential for playacting. This world is almost a microcosm or limited miniature of the worlds outside it — a shadow or echo of all we can create.

Other Spirits

There are many other *spirits* who are not *guides* or *teachers*. Sometimes a *being* is curious and will enter only to view this world and satisfy that curiosity. You would rarely perceive such a *being*.

There are *spirits* who stay on this plane after leaving a body. They usually try to satisfy goals left incomplete. They may go on world tours, watch to see how a project turns out, regard the growth of a child or even an entire family. They cannot actually intervene in any real way but may try to inspire us to take one road over another.

There are *spirits* who sit on top of mountains and contemplate. Others may just waft around and meditate. They have their own reasons for being here.

And then, of course, there are all the different types of *spirits* who live life as animals, plants and other physical universe objects. They are not actually included as a part of this book but are subjects all to themselves.

There are *beings* who have learned how to travel from galaxy to galaxy, perceiving all they can perceive. They rarely ever try to communicate to those in bodies. Their games are different in nature and scope from ours.

No matter how different a *being* may seem, no matter how different his game is to ours, no matter how the physical universe plays tricks on us trying to get us to feel repulsed by each other, no matter all those things.

We are all **one** in spirit and we are all a part of *All There Is* and there are no strangers.

CHAPTER TEN

HOW TO COMMUNICATE WITH YOUR GUIDES AND OTHER SPIRITS

A *spirit guide* is a spirit or entity who is exterior to any physical form, yet relating to the physical world in such a way that makes communication possible. Now, that's a long sentence but, simplistically, that is a good definition of what a *spirit guide* is. The human being is also relating to the *spirit plane(s)* in such a way that makes communication possible. In other words, both entities — the free spirit and the spirit inhabiting physical form — reach toward one another and are able to bridge the reality difference between the two worlds.

In order to communicate with a *spirit*, we must first be able to reach outside of the *physical universe trance state*. It is necessary only to lift slightly out of the solidity of the Earth plane in order to connect with your *spirit friends*.

That which makes communication possible is reality.

There are no easy formulas, no easy rituals, which guarantee communication with your *guides*. There are techniques of relaxation, reverie and meditation which help tremendously. If you use these techniques only — waiting and expecting communication to occur, you will wait and wait and nothing will happen. But if you reach out with *Reality* to the existence of spirit, light and love, while using these techniques, then they will most assuredly work for you.

We must do our part. We can reach the point at which we "know" they are there. If we go about it with the idea of "I'll do this and see what happens," we are quite unlikely to have success.

Remember, now, we are each a part of all communication we receive, and that is never more true than when we are communicating with our *guides*. Our contribution also includes a certain amount of willingness and surrender to the subtle, soft, telepathic voice of the *spirit*. Each time we hear that voice and deny its validity, we are postponing the time when we will experience that wonderful communication and all the love and compassion that comes with it.

One thing that is difficult sometimes to realize is that we are worthy of their attention, their love and regard. They view us as the pure, magnificent, courageous beings we are. Life on this plane is exceedingly difficult and we are held in high esteem for our valiant involvement with it.

What Is Channeling?

Channeling is the result of surrendering with the certain knowledge that a *being* or *beings* are communicating from another plane and that we can bring that communication into the physical universe through our own minds and bodies and relate those communications to ourselves and others.

These communications can come through as intuition, a certain "feeling" about an event (past, present or future); they can come through in the form of inner-silent-audible sounds or inner-visible words or pictures. (These descriptions are made in this manner in order to describe almost impossible-to-describe concepts concerning the receipt of communications from other realms.) Communications can come through the mouth as words without any perception of the form as sent. They can come through when we write (without thinking) in our notebooks after asking questions. They rarely come without our invitation, although they have been known to impinge upon us, asking us to receive.

No matter in what form they come, they are easy sometimes to deny. They are soft, often subtle, and feel much as though we are thinking them on our own. Perhaps the biggest problem is in letting the communication stand for itself and acknowledge it. Once you have, you will love it. You will feel great joy when you *channel*. The degree and quality of that kind of sharing is so beautiful and fulfilling that you will soon lose all possible doubt as to its reality in truth.

Contacting the Inner Beingness of Others

Whatever the existence assumed at present, we can still always contact one another. We can even contact the *inner being* of any member of our family, friends, acquaintances or anyone at all. When one contacts the *inner beingness* of one who is living life in physical form in the present, the communication will most probably be of a very spiritual, loving nature and not one conducive to asking questions or deriving conclusions that exclude the self-determined consciousness of the personality that is inhabiting a body at the time.

For example: We cannot go to the *inner being* of a person in the hopes of convincing them to change their minds in an argument or to place their wishes and desires for actions to be taken in physical life against their own willingness. We cannot make hypnotic suggestions to the *inner beingness* and expect it to work, unless those suggestions coincide with the inner desires of the *being* to whom we are communicating.

When we speak of communicating to an *inner beingness* or to a *spirit guide*, we are speaking of contacting a part of life that is intimately on terms with *All There Is* and, therefore, more understanding of your desires than you are yourself (i.e., in your present state).

It is unreal to think of communicating with another's *inner beingness*, then going to them the next day and saying, "You told me last night that it is perfectly all right for me to keep the lawn mower I borrowed because you have money to buy a new one and I don't." Get the idea? The *inner beingness* of each of us is not intimately interested in Earthly, societal matters unless they concern growth and connecting with *All There Is*.

When people feel close and loving, at one with each other; when they sense the greater part of themselves and others, they are most certainly in contact with the *inner beingness* of themselves and those with whom they have that feeling. Such communion is beautiful and to be prized and nurtured.

"Timing" and Messages

Sometimes we may feel we are getting messages from those humans with whom we have a feeling of closeness or great regard. Such communications are not uncommon and occur much more frequently than we realize. Just because a person was occupied with something entirely engrossing and is sure that he did not "think" of another person at the exact time the communication was received does not mean it did not occur.

Outside the confines of our physical realm there is no time. Communications can be sent at odd moments, only half-formed, to be received when the other person is receptive and come through as a fully formed thought at the receipt point. Realize, now, that we are each a part of all the communication we receive, and for a communication to be complete it is also created in part by the receiver. We sometimes send messages of comfort, support and strength in our sleep, for the other to receive them perhaps two days later while driving to work.

Communication sent out will arrive when the other *being* is ready or receptive to it. Depending upon their perception, they will recognize the sender or not.

Communications from Spirits Still in Physical Universe Trance States

Let's take a moment to look at other kinds of communication. Suppose we are *channeling*, and information of fearful nature comes through. Intimations of danger, of threat or dread of an action have us in a quandary or feeling fearful or anxious. We are experiencing *channeling* all right, but we are *channeling* a *being* who is still playing games in **this physical universe**.

Once we leave the *physical universe trance state* we are no longer fearful. We no longer have great interest in what happens to games we set up while in a body. We no longer have interest in who marries the boss's daughter, or the heiress, or who takes over the company. Get the idea? So if information comes through on that level, we can take it for granted that the *being* is not communicating from the *astral plane*.

There are lower *physical universe trance states* that mimic or echo the *astral plane*. Certain out-of-body experiences occur on such planes. It depends upon which direction one goes when leaving the body — **out** of the body or **exterior** to the body brings one simply from a viewpoint of being in a body to a viewpoint of being out of the body while still very much **in** the physical universe and its trance states.

Two Directions out of the Body

If the attention is directed inward to one's inner universe, the window to the *astral plane* is opened and we become exterior. We are exterior to the physical universe itself.

We can experience out-of-body episodes, seeing what we supposed was present on the *astral plane*, yet still be very much **in** the *physical universe trance states*. One way we can be sure of the difference is in what we encounter. If we encounter **exactly** what we thought we would, we are more than likely not on the *astral plane*, but projecting a world we wanted to see. Once really on the *astral plane*, our realities become changed and we actually begin to remember *Real Reality*. Things begin to seem exceedingly familiar and we feel at home with what we perceive. The experience is very similar to those who come out of a faint, or out of any sort of state of unconsciousness, and look around and begin to put the pieces together, realizing where they are. They relate to the surroundings positively because they recognize the environment and it is not strange to them.

Now, because we are in trance states while on this physical plane, when we come out and into the *astral plane realities*, we are literally coming out of unconsciousness.

We do not have to communicate with any *being* who flies by and wants to tell us which horse will win or where to find gold. They are many times not any more reliable than the loudmouth sitting in a bar. They may be just as giddy, actually thinking they **can** do what they say. Our *guides*, on the other hand, are most probably not a bit interested in where to find gold or which horse will win.

These *beings* who assert their *knowingness* are many times really exerting a sense of humor and love to play jokes. They are not "evil" or bent upon "attacking" us or harming us in any way. We only have to respond with humor and they usually decide to leave us alone.

At any rate, there is nothing to worry about. The only reason they bother us at all is because we are curious about them and **think** they may have some power over us or have something to offer us.

Communications with *beings* can be some of the most rewarding experiences we can have. All *beings* are interesting and wonderful. All *beings* are a part of us and no *being* can really harm another *being*. He can change one's game, but then, that change is being sought by the "victim" or it would not occur.

The main thing is to go unafraid into the stream of life and experience it fully and enjoy all communication as that which *beings* love to do as much as they ever enjoyed anything.

One State at a Time

It is suggested that when one is starting out, practicing these states, only one state be practiced at a time. Start with the **First State**. Get comfortable with it and use it several times before going deeper. Do this with each subsequent state. Get very comfortable with each one. There is the possibility of going too quickly into the deeper states and missing the mark. It isn't dangerous. Nothing we do is dangerous, but it can be unsettling and uncomfortable. It can cause headaches and nausea if not taken step-by-step. Do it properly, not being in a rush and you will reap the rewards.

Exercises

As an aid to creating a climate for communication, practice the following: lie on your back or sit comfortably in a chair with eyes closed. Be still and comfortable and get the idea of relaxing, yet staying alert. Next, clear or clean the space around you by making sweeping motions with your mind, or use a screen made of energy, bringing it up through the floor and on up through the ceiling to about two hundred feet above the house. This will prepare a clean space for *channeling*. The screen or sweeping of the mind will clean out all "negative" masses that may be hanging around. It works by intention. And it really works. Sometimes the room will decidedly lighten up visibly, but that is not always what happens. If the space is very muddy at the start, it will be more noticeable. If it is already relatively clean, it will not be visibly evident.

When the space has been "cleaned," it is easier to create the necessary certainty that the communication you are receiving is indeed from your own *guides* or *friends* rather than from another source. Once in a while it may seem that you are communicating well and a negative message or fearful type of communication will come through. That is a sure sign that someone is playing games with you and that you are not actually tuned in only to your *guides*. Do not worry. These mischievous entities are easily handled and their attention is diverted to other interests. All one has to do is laugh, recognize that they are there and, with intention, sweep them out much the same as cleaning the space. Such entities have very little power and very little actual wish to cause trouble. They are not to be feared. They respond to firmness and will vacate your space quickly. More than likely they are just trying to make you laugh by telling you terrible untruths about yourself. The more certainty you have gained in your communications with your *friends*, the easier it is to keep such entities from entering. After a few successful communications, you should experience no more interruptions.

You can be sure that any negative communications are not coming from your *friends*. There are times when negative communications come from our own minds, revealing how we feel about ourselves. These thoughts will go away if we use the same process as for prankish *beings*. Simply laugh and sweep those thoughts out with your mind.

First State

Now that the stage is set, the space "cleaned," we are ready for the next step. With eyes closed, lean the head back so that the top of the head is as near parallel to the spine as is comfortably possible. Leave it there for about two seconds and slowly lift it back to a straightforward position. (This obviously has to be done sitting up.) If you raise your head too slowly, you may miss the desired effect. One could count to six, perhaps taking one second per count or five to six seconds altogether. When this has been accomplished, you will feel a slight light-headedness. This is because the energy vortex at the top of the head and the point between and slightly above the eyes, sometimes referred to as the **third eye** through which *channeling* enters easily, have been opened. (These energy vortexes are referred to as **chakras** in certain Eastern practices.)

One can *channel* through this state. It is an extremely light altered state and "feels" familiar and comfortable, although slightly more relaxed than usual. This is the state in which we can *channel* when we are alone and are asking questions of our *guides* and *friends*. This is also the best state to aim for if we are in a hurry or if we are extremely disturbed. At these times the deeper states may be more difficult to assume. Sometimes we may go deeper into the *physical universe trance states* — although that is very easy to recognize and we can come right out again. In these cases, we have simply gone in the wrong direction. Remember to always go **inward**.

Now, as we go into these states, we are literally coming **out** of trance, although it may feel we are going deeper as we come up into "higher" states. It is all a matter of agreeing upon the language used.

We may also describe the "higher" states as "deeper" states, still meaning they are taking us **out** of trance into *Real Reality*.

Writing and Conversation

This **First State** is the ideal state to use for writing your *channelings* as they come through and for "conversational" *channeling*. By that, we mean opening up to your *friends* while in meetings or planning ahead with others. We can be inspired with ideas and insights at these times.

This state is also usually done with the eyes open after the initial head positions have been done. One can use the pendulum more easily and accurately while in this state.

Dowsing

The *First State* is perfect for dowsing, and many dowsers unconsciously use it. It is especially effective while map-dowsing. It is a comfortable and easy state with which to focus our concentrations of mental energies without it being noticeable to others. We can operate in this trance state and hold concentration easily without anyone knowing it.

Focused Concentration

Mathematicians, students and scientists use the *First State* all the time. It is widely used by many who never realize they are in an "altered state." Any time we need focused concentration we tend to fall into this state, even without the use of the head positions at the start. These positions make the state more controllable and slightly deeper, however.

In a very true sense, we are **more aware** in this state because we have focused **most** of our attention upon one thing, and of that one thing we are **acutely** aware. Other factors will recede into the background, however.

Not Fragile

These states may feel very fragile at first. We may feel we must slur our words. We may feel slightly inebriated. Let us assure you, although you "feel" as you do, the actual truth is that you can speak even more clearly, relating to this world with great insight and understanding. You can not only speak while in these states but you can open your eyes, walk around and never really lose your concentration. The only exception is in *direct channeling* — while another entity is using your body through which to communicate directly. Even in these cases, the *being* might wish to walk around.

Very quickly, we find the *First State* occurring instantly without using the head position at all. We may even begin to operate in this state constantly, making it a natural part of our everyday state of consciousness.

The *First State* not only opens the vortex at the top of the head but also the smaller vortex in the center of the forehead. That is why this is the ideal state to employ for thinking things through, for memorizing, for imagining as well as *channeling*.

Second State

Begin as in the *First State*. When you have accomplished that, you are ready to launch into deeper states.

Take a deep breath through the nose, letting it out through the mouth. Now, on a second deep breath, **blow** the air out the mouth while looking inward to a spot just behind the throat. This action opens the energy vortex at the throat. You are now in the **Second State**. After assuming this state a number of times you can get into it more directly. Simply execute the head positions and, while blowing the first breath out, focus inward behind the throat, and you are there. This action releases inabilities to allow speech to come through. This is a beautiful state to use while correcting speech impediments.

You will feel yourself relaxing more as you enter this state. The only real difference in these two states is the degree to which one has come into the upper *physical universe trance states*. Each state brings you closer to *Real Reality* and the ability to view life as it really is.

The farther you focus down the body, the deeper the trance state, and the higher the *Reality*.

Third State

For the next deeper state, after having completed the two above, focus behind the heart. The deep breaths as above are conducive to pulling you deeper into trance. The deeper the trance, the less likely are you to encounter *beings* whom you have not invited.

The heart energy vortex is opened and now this is a good state from which to *channel* a *being* in the company of others who would like to ask questions. You can reach out for specific *friends* or put out a call to anyone who would like to answer the question. One can open the eyes in this state or not, as wished.

It is through this area that our love flows in and out. The heart is the place where we concentrate upon finding and communicating with our *inner beingness* and *All There Is*. Looking inward through this point opens us up to all the potentials of life as we wish it to be.

Surrender

The main thing in all these exercises is to surrender yourself to whatever comes through. It is easy, when one is new to *channeling*, to "throw away" words and concepts, being afraid to trust that they are not made up by oneself. It is better to take a chance on it than to throw it away. It will soon be evident if it is a true communication or not. It is difficult to judge by the first few words or sentences.

In the first two states the use of a notebook in which to write the communications as they come through is suggested. Communications which come in through trance are difficult to remember; so writing them down is advised.

It is noticeable that the quality of the communications will improve the more you *channel*. *Channeling* creates fertile ground for increased awareness and as we grow, so does the quality of the communication. We never receive information or answers that are totally beyond our ability to understand. We may have to study the communications before we are really conversant with the concepts, but we are always able to finally assimilate the data.

This is an excellent state with which to seek inspiration from ourselves or our *guides* in regard to very important decisions we wish to make. It is also useful for creative thinking of all kinds as well as creative imagining. This is our natural daydreaming state. So you see, these are not foreign to you.

Fourth State

After having attained the *Third State* one can go farther. With deep breaths to aid you, bring your consciousness down to the area of the solar plexus, opening that energy vortex. The quality of communication from that level can take any one of several forms. The deeper the trance, the less chance of "filtering" the information coming through.

Now again, one can open the eyes or not. The deeper we go, the greater the opportunity for contacting "important" information. This is not a stringent rule by any means, but reflects the degree of surrender necessary in order to accomplish greater communication.

Fifth State

Going even deeper from the *Fourth State*, using again the breaths to help pull your consciousness deeper, focus upon a spot behind the navel. Such focus brings you into a very deep trance in which one can *channel* a *being* openly, using one's own voice. The *channel* has moved out of the body into a serene and productive state toward reaching *inner beingness*.

One will *channel* in this state only if one wishes. No *being* can step in and take over your body unless you wish it. Most *guides* would rather not. They have to come very close to the *physical universe trance states* and in doing so, they **also** begin to experience the pressures of this universe.

This is a wonderful state and can be used for many kinds of meditations with great success. It is especially good for becoming more aware of one's inner life and inner *knowingness*.

It is possible that one would find this state difficult as a vehicle for "direct" *channeling*. It varies with the individual just how deep a trance is necessary for this to happen.

Sixth State

Here we come to the deep state on the sixth level. Using the other states, breathe and let the breath carry you into the spot behind the pubic area near the tailbone. When this vortex is opened, we are in the deepest trance state available through the vortexes of the body.

This state is tremendously relaxed, and opening the eyes is uncomfortable and does distract from this concentration.

This is a perfect state for meditation and for aiding us to sleep. Information gathered in this state is usually filtered much less, and surrendering is more easily accomplished. This state lies at the **top** of the *physical universe trance states*. We can relate beautifully to *Real Reality* from this state. We can communicate with **any** *being* through this state.

The deeper the state, the more one forgets later what was said. Taping is a good practice while *channeling* on this level. Now, the "forgetter" mechanism is natural to this plane. It is part of the reason why we can experience things convincingly, so this is not a negative concept.

We do forget, but if it is recorded, we can bring it back with us. This is why dreams are so hard to remember. They come from out of this dimension and, in an attempt to remember them, we clothe them in physical universe symbols to use as translations into the life and language of this plane.

Seventh State

After the assuming of the states above, we are ready to launch out of this universe completely. When we go into deeper states from this viewpoint we need not worry that we will slide into the lower *physical universe trance states*.

In our own inner world there is complete safety. Here is familiar ground and if we have accomplished the earlier states by looking **inward**, we will be in direct contact with the lower levels of the *astral plane*. We are then **out** of the *physical universe trance state*, still able, however, to relate to the physical universe and its symbols. We are then in close proximity to the state from which our *guides* communicate through us in "direct" *channeling*.

This state is conducive to great insight. It is wise to enter this state in an environment that will not be interruptive. The shock of coming too quickly back into the body can be uncomfortable and unsettling for several hours. Going back into trance helps to return more easily to one's own feeling of equilibrium.

Techniques and Deep States

There are deeper states, but for our purposes we do not need to describe them. There are also different ways in which to reach the states here described. These do seem to bring one quickly into a desired state.

If you are already using a technique for getting into states which work for you, then it is unnecessary to use the ones we have here. You will discover after practicing these techniques that you can start with the *First State* and go on to the *Sixth State* in one fast swoop. You will discover your own most comfortable state and speed as well. Remember, there is nothing cut-and-dried in the *spirit world* and you are indeed delving into the *spirit world* when you are going into trance or looking inward to your own private universe. There is no technique senior to your own way of communicating with your inner world. There is no one greater than you or more adept than you when it comes to knowing yourself. It may seem otherwise when we feel lost and unsure of ourselves. Books and lectures can help inspire us, but finally **we are the ones** who make the journey. No one can make it for us. It is not a matter of you attaining **the** state that permits *channeling* to occur, but rather attaining **your** *channeling* state. The state that is necessary for **you** to attain your own level of surrender to the soft voices of your *friends* is the state you are to look for.

There is absolutely no way possible to judge or evaluate the exact state of another, no matter what the appearances may be. A very perceptive person may be able to aid another in attaining their own personal states, but there is no measuring device that can discover the state of consciousness of another. We can, however, find ourselves sharing parts of the consciousness of another. We can "feel" the oneness of thought, mind and spirit. The feeling is usually intense and beautiful.

Sharing

Eventually, after *channeling* for a time, we will begin simply to **share** thoughts with our *guides* and others. There will be no sense of a *being* "moving in" on our electrical fields. They will just **be** there. We can then draw upon knowledge and wisdom without needing to know the name of the *being* with whom we are speaking. There will be a true sharing of knowledge and viewpoints. We will be drawing upon many viewpoints at once.

It is as though we finally tap into an interdimensional font of knowledge or vast library in which all knowledge is stored.

Results of Channeling

What actually happens is that after *channeling* successfully for a while, we then begin to connect more and more with our own *inner beingness* and from that viewpoint we reach out for *knowingness*. All knowledge, truth and *Reality* lie within each of us. When we finally reach for and connect with our **inner selves**, we have tapped into our most valuable resource.

Realize that when we are in our "original" state, everything exists for us. We are truly a part of *All There Is* — In other words, **we are. We exist**.

In order for truth to exist at all, we have to postulate nontruth. With the introduction of a nontruth, creation is involved. Once an idea, thought or manifestation of any kind is created, it becomes existent. Everything that exists, then, is true. Everything that is imagined is true.

Now we come to the idea of *Reality*. There are truths which exist in a single dimension only and are not even translatable interdimensionally.

For instance, not even the **idea** of separateness can be translated to any but physical universes.

"Chronic" State Changes

Once we have attained these trance states in order to *channel*, we soon find that our ordinary, everyday state has changed. We find that we are going about in a light altered state almost all the time. Life takes on a perpetually brighter aspect, is easier to direct, and one feels happier. Now, as a result, when we go into the states as described earlier, we are actually going ever more deeply into our inner worlds, so that our altered states become usual and everyday occurrences. Then we are able to speak with our *friends* in what has now become our ordinary waking state. We no longer have to evoke it to the same degree as at the beginning.

It is important to realize that once these states become every day states, they no longer **feel** like altered states, and our abilities to control our everyday lives are heightened. We are not walking around in a stupor; rather, we feel more **here** than ever before. Our command of our lives becomes easier and our view of the world brighter, and we definitely take on the character of one who is more intelligent and clearheaded and self-assured than before.

From that state we can communicate with *guides* and *friends* on a more equal footing, realizing more and more our own worth. The realization of our own worth comes naturally in higher states of awareness, so as we continue to communicate with our *guides*, we feel less and less the urge to ask questions and more and more the urge to share our growth excitements with them. At the same time, we grow ever more close to our own inner knowing. . .closer to *Real Reality*. This concept is the subject of our next book. We will go into it much more fully and explore the finer points of using altered states to gain insight and certainty as well as regain memory.

Epilogue

Our *friends* invite us to be **subjective** and know ourselves, know what we want in life, learn how to relate to this world and to other *beings* in a way conducive to the fulfillment of our desires and yearnings toward enlightenment, love and understanding.

Communication with our *guides* is a "down home" experience. It is not strange, mystical and filled with mystery, leaving us feeling small and unworthy. It is familiar. It is *Home* and safety, love and acceptance. It is that which helps us connect with our own vastness. Our own greatness. Our own superior *knowingness*.

Live fully, my dear friends, in the knowledge that *All There Is* exists within and for us and that we are truly **not alone**.

Index

NOTES

Also by ACS Publications

All About Astrology Series of booklets
The American Atlas, Expanded Fifth Edition: US Latitudes & Longitudes,
Time Changes and Time Zones (Shanks)
The American Book of Tables (Michelsen)
The American Ephemeris Series 1901-2000
The American Ephemeris for the 20th Century
          [Noon or Midnight] 1900 to 2000, Revised Fifth Edition
The American Ephemeris for the 21st Century 2001-2050, Revised Second Edition
The American Heliocentric Ephemeris 1901-2000
The American Midpoint Ephemeris 1991-1995
The American Sidereal Ephemeris 1976-2000
Asteroid Goddesses: The Mythology, Psychology and Astrology
        of the Reemerging Feminine (George & Bloch)
Astro-Alchemy: Making the Most of Your Transits (Negus)
Astro Essentials: Planets in Signs, Houses & Aspects (Pottenger)
Astrological Games People Play (Ashman)
Astrological Insights into Personality (Lundsted)
Basic Astrology: A Guide for Teachers & Students (Negus)
Basic Astrology: A Workbook for Students (Negus)
The Book of Jupiter (Waram)
The Book of Neptune (Waram)
The Changing Sky: A Practical Guide to the New Predictive Astrology (Forrest)
Complete Horoscope Interpretation:
        Putting Together Your Planetary Profile (Pottenger)
Cosmic Combinations: A Book of Astrological Exercises (Negus)
Dial Detective: Investigation with the 90° Dial (Simms)
Easy Tarot Guide (Masino)
Expanding Astrology's Universe (Dobyns)
Hands That Heal (Burns)
Healing with the Horoscope: A Guide To Counseling (Pottenger)
Houses of the Horoscope (Herbst)
The Inner Sky: The Dynamic New Astrology for Everyone (Forrest)
The International Atlas, Revised Third Edition:
        World Latitudes & Longitudes, Time Changes and Time Zones (Shanks)
The Koch Book of Tables (Michelsen)
Midpoints: Unleashing the Power of the Planets (Munkasey)
New Insights into Astrology (Press)
The Night Speaks: A Meditation on the Astrological Worldview (Forrest)
The Only Way to... Learn Astrology, Vols. I-V (March & McEvers)
        Volume I - Basic Principles
        Volume II - Math & Interpretation Techniques
        Volume III - Horoscope Analysis
        Volume IV- Learn About Tomorrow: Current Patterns
        Volume V - Learn About Relationships: Synastry Techniques
        Volume VI - Learn About Horary and Electional Astrology (Available 5/94)
Planetary Heredity (M. Gauquelin)
Planetary Planting (Riotte)
Planets in Solar Returns: A Yearly Guide for Transformation and Growth (Shea)
Planets in Work: A Complete Guide to Vocational Astrology (Binder)
Psychology of the Planets (F. Gauquelin)
Skymates: The Astrology of Love, Sex and Intimacy (S. & J. Forrest)
Spirit Guides: We Are Not Alone (Belhayes)
Tables of Planetary Phenomena (Michelsen)
Twelve Wings of the Eagle: Our Spiritual Evolution through the Ages of the Zodiac
        (Simms)
The Way of the Spirit: The Wisdom of the Ancient Nanina (Whiskers)

MORE NEW AGE PUBLICATIONS from ACS

Titles from Steven Forrest

The Inner Sky:
The Dynamic New Astrology For Everyone
Forrest's New Astrology encourages free choice—not fate. The author provides directions for uncovering your hidden potential. Nothing is "carved-in-stone" when it comes to your personality—you can change. Forrest skillfully guides you while you seek out and find new areas of inner strength and personal growth. **(B131X) $12.95**

The Changing Sky:
A Practical Guide to the New Predictive Astrology
In this sequel to *The Inner Sky* Forrest dispels the myths and misconceptions that surround predictive astrology. In no uncertain terms the author describes what predictive astrology can do for you and what it cannot. Forrest states… "What modern predictive astrology can do is inform you in advance of the natural rhythms of your life—and moods—thereby helping you arrange your outward experiences in the happiest, most harmonious and efficient manner." **(B122X) $12.95**

Skymates: The Astrology of Love, Sex and Intimacy
Steven and Jodie Forrest have taken pen in hand to put years of their own practical experience about *synastry*—the astrology of intimacy, sex and partnership—into this book. The authors discuss how best to use astrology in your relationship(s)… as "a wise counselor, an all-knowing third party who loves both of us with supernatural clarity, insight, and caring." Steven and Jodie use astrology in a most creative and unique way to help you discover the emotional needs of yourself and your lover. **(B143X) $14.95**

The Night Speaks:
A Meditation on the Astrological Worldview
The Night Speaks, written with Steven Forrest's wonderfully evocative style, elicits awe and inspiration in the reader. He traces the wonder of astrology and the human/cosmos connection. He discusses some scientific information as to why and how we might explain astrology, but keeps throughout a mystical, transcendent feel. If you've wanted a book to explain "why you believe in that stuff" to doubting friends, this is it! **(B149X) $12.95**
